Climbing California's Mountains

Jay Anderson

FALCON®

GUILFORD, CONNECTICUT
HELENA, MONTANA
AN IMPRINT OF THE GLOBE PEQUOT PRESS

A FALCON GUIDE®

Photos are by the author unless otherwise noted.
Maps by Topaz Maps Inc. © The Globe Pequot Press
Topography provided by Maps a la carte, Inc.

Library of Congress Cataloging-in-Publication Data
Anderson, Jay, 1956–
   Climbing California's mountains / Jay Anderson.-- 1st ed.
     p. cm. -- (A Falcon guide)
   Includes index.
   ISBN 0-7627-2210-X
     1. Mountaineering--California--Guidebooks.   2. Mountains--California--Guidebooks. 3. California--Guidebooks. I. Title. II. Series

GV199.42.C2 A63 2003
796.52'2'09794--dc21

                                                              2002026391

Manufactured in the United States of America
First Edition/First Printing

Contents

Preface vii
Acknowledgments viii

INTRODUCTION 1
  Picking the Peaks 1
  Rewards of the Climb 3
  Guides and Climbing Clubs............................5
  Safety in the Mountains 5
  Essential Equipment 7
  Permits 8

HOW TO USE THIS GUIDE 9
  Map Legend..10

NORTHERN CALIFORNIA......................11
  1. Mount Shasta 11
  2. Castle Dome 14
  3. Mount Lassen 16
  4. Eureka Peak...18
  5. Sierra Buttes 21

LAKE TAHOE AREA................................24
  6. Castle Peak 24
  7. Pacific Crest Trail Traverse 26
  8. Mount Tallac..29
  9. Mount Rose..32
  10. Freel Peak...34
  11. Jobs Peak 37
  12. Jobs Sister 40

YOSEMITE NATIONAL PARK.................41
  13. Matterhorn Peak 41
  14. Mount Conness 43

  15. Mount Dana 46
  16. Amelia Earhart Peak 48
  17. Mount Lyell...50
  18. Mount Maclure.......................................52
  19. Cathedral Peak 54
  20. Clouds Rest 56
  21. Half Dome 60

HIGH SIERRA...64
  22. Mammoth Mountain 64
  23. Mount Ritter...66
  24. Banner Peak 68
  25. Mount Morrison 70
  26. Mount Starr 72
  27. Mount Morgan..74
  28. Mount Mills 77
  29. Mount Abbot 77
  30. Mount Dade 80
  31. Mount Tom..82
  32. Basin Mountain 84
  33. Mount Emerson 86
  34. Mount Lamarck 88
  35. Mount Darwin 90
  36. Hurd Peak 92
  37. Mount Gayley 94
  38. Split Mountain.......................................96
  39. Mount Prater 98
  40. Birch Mountain 98
  41. Mount Tinemaha....................................101

MOUNT WHITNEY AREA 104
  42. Kearsage Peak 104

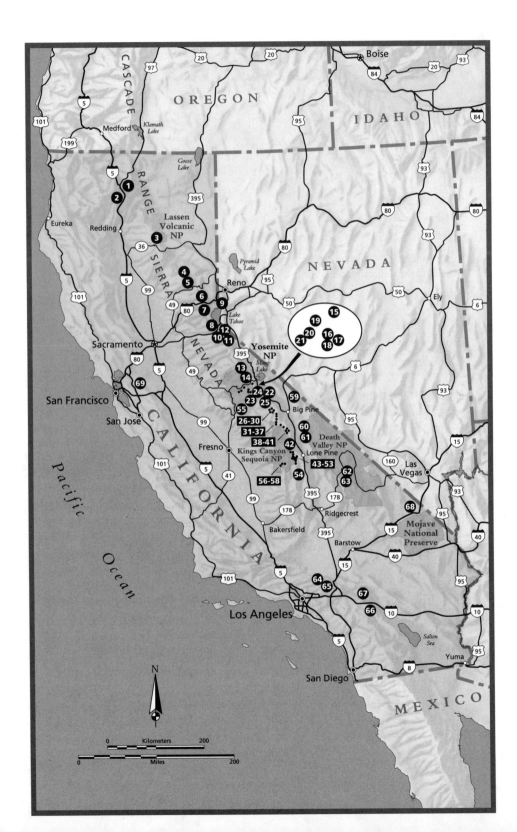

43. Mount Williamson 107
44. Mount Tyndall 109
45. Mount Whitney 111
46. Mount Muir 115
47. Mount Russell 115
48. Lone Pine Peak 118
49. Mount LeConte 120
50. Mount Mallory......................................122
51. Mount Irvine...124
52. Mount Langley 126
53. Cirque Peak..128
54. Olancha Peak 130

WEST OF THE SIERRA CREST 133
55. Fresno Dome...133
56. Sawtooth Peak 135
57. Needham Mountain 137
58. Mineral Peak...140

WHITE MOUNTAINS AND DEATH VALLEY...............................141
59. White Mountain Peak 141
60. Waucoba Mountain.............................143
61. Squaw Peak 147
62. Wildrose Peak.......................................147
63. Telescope Peak 151

SOUTHERN CALIFORNIA 153
64. Mount Baden-Powell...........................153
65. Mount San Antonio 155
66. San Jacinto Peak..................................158
67. San Gorgonio Mountain 160
68. Clark Mountain 162

SAN FRANCISCO AREA........................164
69. Mount Diablo..164

PEAKS AT A GLANCE 167

Help Us Keep This Guide Up to Date

Every effort has been made by the author and editors to make this guide as accurate and useful as possible. However, many things can change after a guide is published—trails are rerouted, regulations change, techniques evolve, facilities come under new management, etc.

We would love to hear from you concerning your experiences with this guide and how you feel it could be improved and kept up to date. While we may not be able to respond to all comments and suggestions, we'll take them to heart and we'll also make certain to share them with the author. Please send your comments and suggestions to the following address:

The Globe Pequot Press
Reader Response/Editorial Department
P.O. Box 480
Guilford, CT 06437

Or you may e-mail us at:

editorial@globe-pequot.com

Thanks for your input, and happy travels!

Preface

I moved to California from Chicago with my parents while I was still in high school, in 1971. I had already climbed and peak-bagged in the Rockies and skied in the Midwest, but I remember that California had a special allure. This was the Golden State, a land of breathtaking mountains, of sun and white granite, the spiritual homeland of John Muir.

Skiing in the Sierra Nevada range, rock climbing on Mount Diablo, backpacking out of Tuolumne Meadows—these became my very reasons for being. A winter solo of Donner Peak, complete with crampons and ice ax, was quite the adventure for a transplanted Midwestern boy. Taking high school chums up Cathedral Peak was another high point. The next summer's adventure—perhaps *misadventure* describes it better—on Mount Whitney's east face taught me the value of acclimatization and gave me a healthy respect for altitude.

As the years went by I became more obsessed with rock climbing and found my way all over the state in a continuing search for new vertical adventures. In the early '90s I relocated to Reno and began doing marathon and ultramarathon trail runs, largely in the Sierra. That provided a whole new perspective on how and why to climb a mountain.

But the more I did in the mountains, the more I realized that it was not the achievements, not the activities themselves, as much as the setting that kept drawing me back. Running, hiking, and climbing were all excuses, or opportunities, to *be* in the mountains. Running along the Pacific Crest Trail in September is not a challenge against a stopwatch, but rather a chance to feel the cool temperatures, to experience the light that defines autumn in the Sierra. Standing on top of Clouds Rest watching thunderheads roll in across Yosemite Valley, while to the north Mount Conness is in sun and to the east Mount Lyell is enshrouded in cloud, is all about enjoying the mountains—and not about how long it took to reach the summit.

This book celebrates the infinite diversity of California's mountains and the experiences they offer to us—from observing a rattlesnake on top of Mount San Antonio while looking out over the Los Angeles basin, to huddling on the summit of Mount Lassen on a chilly afternoon, to spying Catalina Island from San Jacinto Peak, to simply escaping after work up to Mount Diablo. If I can steer hikers and climbers toward new places and new adventures that give them a glimpse of the great scope of mountain ascents available in California, I will have achieved my goal in writing this book.

Acknowledgments

I'd like to thank Jan Cronan for overseeing this project, Don Graydon for his relentless efforts, and John Burbidge for the initial stages. And most of all, special thanks to Liz Schramm for cracking the whip and sticking by me throughout the ups and downs—literally and figuratively—of this long project.

Introduction

In 1863 the California Geological Survey, under Josiah Dwight Whitney, undertook a major survey and exploration of the Sierra Nevada range. The Survey completed the first systematic ascents of many California mountains and created the framework of peak names and geographical provinces that we continue to use today. It also inspired an interest in mountaineering that flowered into the grand tradition that is hiking and climbing among the high peaks of California.

The landscape of California is dizzying in its complexity. That such a diverse and varied land can be arbitrarily contained and defined within the strict geographic boundaries that shape what we call California is evidence of our human need for order, our talent for reducing larger concepts into manageable chunks. In reality, the Mojave Desert blends into the greater Southwest. The northern volcanic zone continues north beyond our political boundaries and into the Cascades of the Pacific Northwest. The peaks of Death Valley and the White Mountains start their way into the basin and range province of the intermountain West.

Only the Sierra Nevada mountains and the state's coastal ranges are entirely within the official bounds of California. And yet we imbue the state with a conformity of purpose, a mind-set—call it California Dreaming.

Picking the Peaks

This book is for those who want to experience the breadth of basic mountain climbing in California. I've selected peaks representing a wide range of difficulty in a variety of settings, avoiding for the most part specialized technical climbing.

I've compiled this collection of peaks using a variety of overlapping criteria. I studied lists of county and range high points, and I considered the pure aesthetics of the shape of the peak and the quality of view. Ease of approach and the quality of the climb itself are key factors. Geographical location was also a consideration. This is a guide to California mountains, so I've included peaks from areas beyond the Sierra Nevada range, generally giving more than one peak per area to make traveling to remote sites more rewarding.

No two lists of the most desirable peaks in California will be the same. For this selection of sixty-nine mountains, I kept a number of factors in mind:

Aesthetics: How does the peak look from afar? Does the sight of the mountain make you want to climb it? This is certainly the case for Mount Shasta, Lone Pine Peak, San Jacinto Peak, Banner Peak, and Mount Ritter.

Ease of approach: One goal of this book is to get you onto accessible peaks; this is not a backpacking guide. It's possible to climb each of the peaks in one day from the trailhead. However, it's true that some of the climbs—such as Mount Williamson, Mount Tyndall, Banner Peak, Mount Ritter, Mount Lyell, and Mount Maclure—are more practical as multiday trips for most parties.

1

Cathedral Peak

Modest difficulty: By and large the climbs described in this book are nontechnical, meaning that for most parties, ropes and other climbing gear will not be necessary. However, a few of the peaks stretch any concept of nontechnical. Cathedral Peak, Mount Williamson, Mount Tyndall, and Castle Dome are best left for more advanced mountaineers with rock-climbing experience, some of whom will want to rope up. Mount Ritter, Mount Shasta, Banner Peak, Mount Lyell, and Mount Maclure are among the peaks that require proficiency in the use of an ice ax and possibly crampons. It is not the purpose of this book to teach the proper use of ropes, protection gear, or snow and ice equipment. You'll have to get such instruction and become proficient in these techniques before embarking on any of the peaks where it is necessary. Or just stick with the majority of the peaks that we'll talk about: Each one of these others makes for a tough but rewarding ascent to a worthy summit, but without the need for you to be a trained mountaineer.

Quality of the climb: For the most part, this means that the climb itself is enjoyable. Romping up San Jacinto Peak or San Gorgonio Mountain, with their changing terrain, is fun at every step. Pulling yourself up the cables on Half Dome is an adventure you won't have anywhere else. Watching Lake Tahoe appear as you crest the final bit of Mount Tallac is likewise unforgettable.

Established routes: Most of these climbs use well-established trails, though some involve off-trail routes, especially as you get closer to the summit. Mount Shasta and Castle Dome, for instance, require routefinding skills. Any required off-trail travel is mentioned in the text of the appropriate write-up.

Views: When it comes to the quality of the views, there isn't a dud in the book. But some stand out: Lone Pine Peak has arguably the best summit view in the Sierra; the Sierra panorama from White Mountain is too good to miss; the view from the top of Telescope Peak includes the highest and lowest points in the contiguous United States.

Mileage: I included climbs of various lengths. You may want to spend the whole day hiking the Mount Langley/Cirque Peak loop. On another day, the short stroll up Fresno Dome might be just what the doctor ordered. There is plenty of variety to suit the mood of any day.

Rewards of the Climb
Each of the summits described in these pages offers its own special reward. Here's my subjective list of some of the best reasons for climbing to particular summits:

Top climbs for the hard-core mountaineer
- Mount Shasta
- Mount Tyndall
- Mount Williamson

Most fun for a rock climber
- Castle Dome
- Cathedral Peak
- Mountaineer's Route on Mount Whitney
- Mount Williamson

Best afternoon romp
- Fresno Dome

Best place to take photos
- Lone Pine Peak (great close-ups of the High Sierra)
- White Mountain (the widest view of Sierra peaks)

Most beautiful wildflowers, in season
- Mount Dana
- San Jacinto Peak
- San Gorgonio Mountain
- Mount Diablo

Finest views from the summit
- Lone Pine Peak
- Mount Shasta
- Telescope Peak

Fastest escape from Los Angeles
- Mount San Antonio

Best view of technical rock climbing
- Half Dome (where climbers may spend days on the vertical northwest face)

Best après-climb swims
- In Donner Lake, after the Pacific Crest Trail Traverse from Donner Pass to Squaw Valley; be bold, it's cold.
- In Lake Tahoe, after the ascent of Mount Tallac; be bolder, it's colder.
- In Tenaya Lake, after the ascent of Cathedral Peak; another frigid beauty.

I happen to be an avid trail runner, and in preparing this book, I ran up and down many of these peaks. For the trail runners in the crowd, let me offer my choices for various kinds of runs:

Easy runs
- Mount Diablo
- Fresno Dome

Short but high runs
- Wildrose Peak
- Mammoth Mountain
- Mount Dana

Moderate runs complicated by altitude
- Eureka Peak
- Sierra Buttes
- Castle Peak
- Mount Baden-Powell

Longer runs of moderate technical difficulty and requiring altitude acclimatization
- Pacific Crest Trail Traverse
- Telescope Peak
- San Gorgonio Mountain
- Mount San Jacinto
- White Mountain
- Amelia Earhart Peak

Long runs, where it's best to be in a marathon frame of mind
- Clouds Rest
- Mount Whitney
- Mount Langley
- Mount Russell
- Mount Tom
- Mount Emerson

Marathon (or greater) runs with significant technical difficulty
- Mount Lyell
- Mount Maclure
- Mount Williamson
- Mount Tyndall

Guides and Climbing Clubs

It can be a good idea to go out with a hiking or climbing club or hire a guide for types of climbs you're not accustomed to. If a climb requires experience in rock climbing or mountaineering that you just don't have, a guide or a climbing club can help make the ascent safely possible for you.

Those with limited mountaineering experience might want to use a guide or travel in a group for ascents of Mount Lyell, Mount Maclure, Mount Shasta, Banner Peak, and Mount Ritter. People with few rock climbing skills will want help on Cathedral Peak, the Mountaineers route on Mount Whitney, and Mount Williamson.

Yosemite Valley and Tuolumne Meadows have full guide services during the summer. A number of guides work out of Bishop, Mammoth, Mount Shasta, and other areas. The Sierra Club, other outdoor organizations, and some colleges and universities sponsor hikes and climbs.

Among the resources for information on guide services are:

- Shasta Mountain Guides; (530) 926-3117; www.shastaguides.com.
- The Sierra Club; (415) 977-5500; www.sierraclub.org/outings
- Southern Yosemite Mountain Guides; (831) 459-8735; www.symg.com.
- United States Mountain Guides Association; www.usmga.net.
- Yosemite Mountaineering School; (209) 372-8344; www.yosemitepark.com/html/mountain.html.

Safety in the Mountains

The peaks of California are sometimes viewed as a gentle bunch, but don't be misled. There are hazards here, and peak hikers must be prepared.

California is not known for afternoon showers but bring rain gear—especially on longer routes and in the spring, fall, and winter. Many California peaks have exposed tops and ridges that are dangerously unsuited for travel during electrical storms. The weather can change wildly during a single day, particularly when a peak involves as much as 8,000 feet of vertical gain.

Beware of hypothermia, the lowering of core body temperature below normal levels. If severe, it prompts such symptoms as slurred speech, poor judgment, and erratic behavior. If not checked, it will eventually lead to mental and physical collapse and death. Most hypothermia occurs in wet conditions, at temperatures between 30 and 50 degrees Fahrenheit, and comes on gradually, often imperceptibly. Treat by putting on warm, dry clothes and drinking hot liquids. Extreme cases are generally treated by putting the victim in a dry sleeping bag with another person. Better to prevent than to have to treat: Stay dry and warm, and be alert for erratic behavior in chilly conditions.

Watch out for overheating, too. Pace yourself in hot weather and drink plenty of water. Heat exhaustion is characterized by flushing, sweating, and fatigue. Rest and water are the antidotes. Heat stroke is much more serious. Symptoms include extreme paleness and a lack of sweat. Immediate medical attention is necessary.

Boulder fields, Mount San Antonio

Altitude sickness brings on symptoms that include headaches, stomachaches, general lassitude, and lack of appetite. It generally occurs from gaining altitude too fast, but can happen anytime at altitudes as low as 4,000 or 5,000 feet. Aspirin and water help, as well as rest and a slower pace. In severe cases, descending is the only way to deal with it. Try to acclimate for a few days before climbing above 10,000 feet or so, especially if coming from sea level.

Drink plenty of water. Exercise physiologists say you need to drink as much as eight ounces every fifteen minutes during vigorous exercise (a quart every hour) to maintain normal functions. While that amount may be impractical, the point is well taken. Staying hydrated will help in dealing with heat and altitude.

Purify your drinking water. All water in streams, creeks, springs, and snowmelt must be assumed to contain *Giardia* or other noxious biota, such as liver flukes. Boil it, treat it with one of the many commercially available chemical preparations, or pump it through a proven filter.

Many California peaks are in black-bear country. Most problems revolve around bears wanting human food or humans getting between mother bears and their cubs. Bears are generally not aggressive, but they're immensely strong and nearly unstoppable. Campers in Yosemite can be issued citations for improper food storage, and in the Mammoth Lakes backcountry, bear-proof food canisters are mandated for backpackers. Store your food properly. Except where canisters are mandated, this generally means hanging the food from a tree with a rope. Give bears space, and especially stay away from sows with cubs. Never try to retrieve anything from a bear.

Mountain lions are a different problem. Generally secretive and stealthy, they have been known to be aggressive. There are no heavy lion populations in the vicinity of any of the peaks in this book, but the lion population is rising, and large-cat awareness is something to keep in mind. If confronting a mountain lion, look as large as possible, raise arms and coats over your head, and fight back if necessary. Running away may trigger an attack response.

Scorpions, spiders, centipedes, and other poisonous creatures produce venom that affects people to varying degrees. Watch where you put your hands, and shake out your shoes in the morning. I am a veteran of tick fever, a scorpion sting, and various bug bites, and I'm not interested in repeating these experiences.

Rattlesnakes are a largely avoidable hazard. Though a lot of sounds, such as rustling leaves, suggest the rattle of a snake, the sound is distinctive; you will know it when you hear it, even if you have never heard it before. Give them room, and you should have no problem. They are most likely to be encountered at dusk after hot days. They are most common in the desert and foothill areas but are rarely seen above seven thousand feet.

Before you set out on any outdoor adventure, know yourself. Realistically assess your physical condition. Cardiovascular fitness is the most important consideration, but knowledge of how to deal with heat, cold, and altitude, and knowing how much you can realistically do in a day, is invaluable. When in doubt, err on the side of discretion. Allow plenty of time, and don't push yourself to the point of exhaustion.

Among the Internet sources that provide information on outdoors topics including mountain safety are:

- www.hikercentral.com: a site with links to all manner of outdoor-related survival topics, including the weather, animals, lightning, and hypothermia.
- http://members.aol.com/hikenet/introtc.html: a site with links to hiking clubs and other resources.
- www.geocities.com/yosemite/falls/9200/backpacking_and_hiking.html: information on hiking.
- www.rayjardine.com: Ray Jardine's home page, with a very different take on lightweight backpacking.

Also helpful are the books in the *Basic Essentials* series from The Globe Pequot Press, including texts on avalanche safety, use of map and compass, use of GPS units, survival skills, wilderness first aid, and bears.

Essential Equipment

Essential equipment is the gear you need to carry to get you safely through an ascent, without it being excessively burdensome. Here is a list of some essentials (in addition to food and water) for most day climbs:

- Proper footwear, usually comfortable, lightweight hiking boots or trail shoes. If snow travel is expected, you'll want more substantial boots.
- Emergency bivouac gear, specific for the weather conditions expected
- Rain gear
- Warm clothing as needed
- Matches

- Map and compass. A global positioning system (GPS) receiver is not a substitute for map and compass, because it won't always work in heavy brush or narrow canyons, the batteries can wear out, and water can damage it—but such a unit can be handy and useful.
- Sunscreen
- First-aid kit and the knowledge to use it
- Hat
- Specialized equipment specific for the peak, weather, and time of year. Depending on conditions, you may need such items as an ice ax, crampons, snowshoes, extra bivy gear, or bear-proof food canisters.
- Camera. OK, so it's not an essential, but you'll be glad you have it.

Permits

Many California peaks require permits for day and/or overnight use and for parking. All cars parked on national forest land in Southern California are required to display a parking pass ($5.00 for a day, $30.00 for a year). Known as an Adventure Pass, it is available at federal and state ranger stations.

Mount Shasta requires a permit and a separate summit fee, handled on a self-service basis at the trailhead—but an additional overnight permit and fee must be secured at the Mount Shasta Ranger Station (204 West Alma Street, Mount Shasta, CA 96067; 916-926-4511).

The Mount Whitney region has its own idiosyncrasies, discussed in the Mount Whitney Area section of this book. Further information is available from the Mount Whitney Ranger Station (640 South Main Street, Lone Pine, CA 93545; 760-876-6200).

Peaks in federally managed areas require a permit, kept in the possession of the hiker, for overnight visits. They are available at federal ranger stations. Permits are normally not required for day use.

Selected sources of additional permit information:

Northern California
- Plumas National Forest, 159 Lawrence Street, Quincy CA 95971; (888) 822-3119.

Lake Tahoe Area
- Lake Tahoe Basin Management Unit, (530) 573-2694.
- Lake Tahoe Visitor Center, (530) 573-2674.
- Tahoe National Forest, 631 Coyote Street, Nevada City CA 95959.

Yosemite National Park
- Wilderness Permits, P.O. Box 545, Yosemite CA 95389; (209) 372-0740; www.nps.gov/yose/wilderness/permits.htm.

High Sierra and White Mountains
- White Mountain Ranger Station, 798 North Main Street, Bishop CA 93514; (760) 873-2500.
- www.thehighsierra.com (then click on *permits*).

How to Use This Book

Climbing California's Mountains is divided into geographic areas. Within each area are write-ups on individual peaks, accompanied by photos and maps to help in navigation. For each climb, you'll find key information under a series of headings, including the following.

Highlights: Reasons for undertaking the climb; what makes it special.

Distance: Round-trip mileage for each climb, including an estimation of the distance on trails and the distance off of trails.

Difficulty: Difficulty of the climb, rated both by a number that indicates the class of difficulty and by an adjective that describes the overall effort involved.

The numbered class ratings are:

- Class 1: Walking uphill.
- Class 2: Walking uphill, sometimes off-trail, with hands occasionally used for balance.
- Class 3: Travel where the use of your hands is required to aid in the climbing.
- Class 4: The beginning level of technical rock climbing; some parties will want a rope and climbing equipment. The hardest routes in this book have brief Class 4 sections
- Class 5: Technical climbing, with rope and other gear mandatory. None of the climbs in this book are rated Class 5.

The climbs are also rated as easy, moderate, strenuous, or very strenuous, taking into consideration such factors as altitude, elevation gain, harshness of terrain, and mileage.

The two ratings work together to give a balanced picture of the climb's difficulty. For example, Mount Whitney by the main trail is technically easy (Class 1), but as a hike of 21 miles round trip with an elevation gain of 6,000 feet, it is strenuous. The Cathedral Peak climb is more difficult technically (Class 4), but the mileage is less than a third of that for Mount Whitney so it is listed as moderate.

Best Months: In general, the best climbing season for a given peak. However, be aware that unusual storms or a heavy snowpack can make for difficult conditions in even these months.

Maps: Specific maps that are useful for the climb. USGS topographic maps are published by the U.S. Geological Survey and are available at ranger stations, map stores, and most outdoors supply stores. The maps are also offered on CD ROM.

DeLorme topographic maps are published by the DeLorme company (P.O. Box 298, Yarmouth, ME, 04096; 207–846–7000; www.delorme.com). The maps useful for this book are included in one of three DeLorme publications: *Northern California Atlas and Gazetteer* (fifth edition), *Southern and Central California Atlas and Gazetteer* (fifth edition), or *Nevada Atlas and Gazetteer* (first edition). Older editions may use somewhat different page numbers. These atlases are available at most outdoors stores and many bookstores.

Tom Harrison maps, based on USGS maps, are printed on a foldable, water-resistant material. They are sold at many outdoors stores, or check www.tomharrisonmaps.com for selection and availability.

National Geographic maps also are useful, especially the one for Yosemite. This map is sold in Yosemite, or check at http://shop.nationalgeographic.com.

Permits: Specific permits required for use of each area.

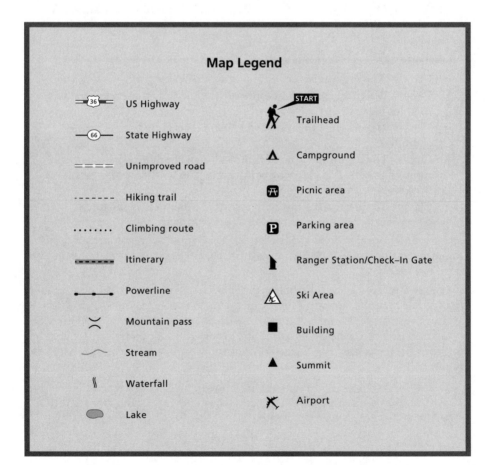

Map Legend

US Highway		Trailhead
State Highway		Campground
Unimproved road		Picnic area
Hiking trail		Parking area
Climbing route		Ranger Station/Check–In Gate
Itinerary		Ski Area
Powerline		Building
Mountain pass		Summit
Stream		Airport
Waterfall		
Lake		

Northern California

The Northern California region of this book extends from the Oregon border down to the Sierra Buttes, north of Lake Tahoe. The northernmost section of this region includes Mount Shasta and Mount Lassen, volcanic peaks that mark the southern extremity of the Cascade range that runs up through Oregon and Washington. Also here is Castle Dome, a granitic peak southwest of Shasta. The landscape is of low, wooded hillsides, with the high mountains providing a dramatic topographic contrast.

South of Mount Lassen lie Plumas and Sierra Counties, with rolling, mountainous terrain informally known as the Northern Sierra. Not as high as the mountains to the north or south, it features open vistas and a sea of Jeffrey and ponderosa pines. The two peaks included in this section—Eureka Peak and Sierra Buttes—offer views extending from Lake Tahoe to the south to Mount Lassen to the north. The stark panorama of the desert to the east contrasts with California's fertile Central Valley to the west. Both peaks afford straightforward logistics, steep climbing, and fewer crowds in season than at many of the more sought-after Sierra summits.

1. MOUNT SHASTA

Highlights: The highest point in Northern California. You'll find mixed terrain, from forest to rocky slopes to snowfields. This is a long, physical trek, all the more satisfying for the effort needed to attain the summit, with its unparalleled views.

Distance: 14 miles round trip (almost all on a trail).

Difficulty: Class 3; strenuous; crampons and ice ax needed.

Trailhead Elevation: 6,800 feet

Summit Elevation: 14,162 feet

Elevation Gain: 7,362 feet

Best Months: March through July.

Maps: USGS Mount Shasta; DeLorme *Northern California Atlas and Gazetteer*, page 36.

Latitude: 41°24'34"N

Longitude: 122°11'38"W

Permits: Self-service registration required at the Bunny Flat trailhead for day use; $15 fee for each person climbing above 10,000 feet. For overnight wilderness permits (additional fee), contact the Mount Shasta Ranger Station, open 8:00 A.M. to 4:30 P.M. Monday through Friday; 204 West Alma Street, Mount Shasta, CA 96067; (916) 926–4511.

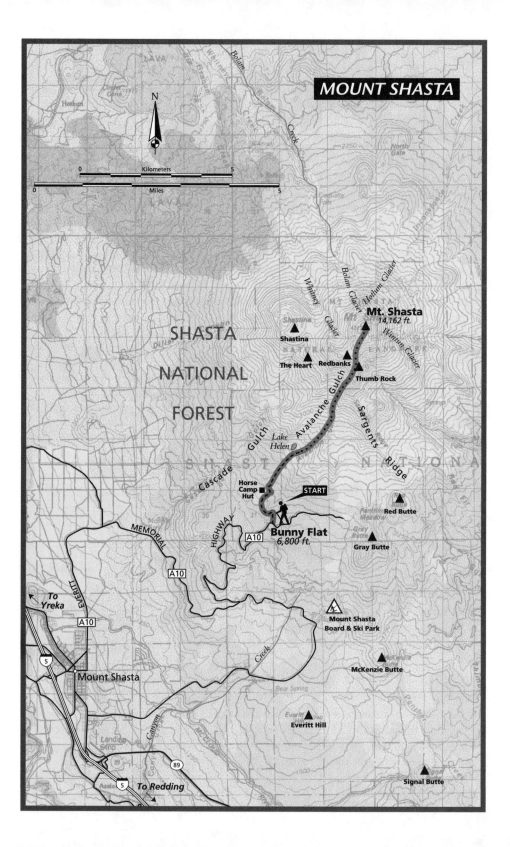

MOUNT SHASTA

N

Kilometers
0 — 5

Miles
0 — 5

SHASTA

NATIONAL

FOREST

LAVA

Whitney Creek

Bolam Creek

North Gate

Inconstance Creek

Mud Creek

Whitney Glacier

Bolam Glacier

Hotlum Glacier

Mt. Shasta
14,162 ft.

Winton Glacier

▲ *Shastina*
Shastina

The Heart

▲ **Redbanks**

▲ **Thumb Rock**

Avalanche Gulch

Sargents Ridge

Cascade Gulch

Lake Helen ○

Horse Camp Hut ■

START

Bunny Flat
6,800 ft.

[A10]

HIGHWAY

MEMORIAL

EVERITT

[A10]

[A10]

To Yreka

[5]

Mount Shasta

To Redding

[5]

[89]

McCloud Creek

Bear Spring

Panther Meadow

▲ **Red Butte**

Gray Butte

▲ **Gray Butte**

⚡ **Mount Shasta Board & Ski Park**

▲ **McKenzie Butte**

▲ **Everitt Hill**

▲ **Signal Butte**

Trailhead: Bunny Flat. From the town of Mount Shasta, off Interstate 5, go northeast on Lake Street from the intersection of Lake Street and Mount Shasta Boulevard. After a half-mile, turn left on Everitt Memorial Highway. Follow this windy road 11.5 miles to the Bunny Flat trailhead.

Mount Shasta is the undisputed queen of Northern California. A dormant shield volcano at the southern end of the Cascade Range, the mountain rises to 14,162 feet from rolling country that is only a couple of thousand feet above sea level. This great local relief makes it a dramatic and picturesque peak, the most prominent landmark for hundreds of miles. The views from the summit are sweeping: the Cascade Mountains to the north, Mount Lassen to the southeast, the Coast ranges to the west, and the Central Valley to the south.

The easiest way up Mount Shasta (and the route of the first ascent) is the Avalanche Gulch route. It was first climbed by a group led by Capt. E. D. Pierce on August 14, 1854. There is a voluntary feces carryout policy in the Avalanche Gulch area; poop bags are available at the trailhead.

This route can be done in one very long day (twelve to fourteen hours or more) or broken up into two or three days with bivouacs at Lake Helen. One-day parties often leave as early as two or three in the morning. It's possible to climb Mount Shasta all year-round, though it takes a hardy soul to head up in the cold of winter. The route usually requires crampons and ice ax any time of year. Rockfall can be especially dangerous in August, when the snowpack is at its smallest and loose rocks are most prevalent. In addition, ascents in August and September can be slowed considerably because much travel will be on loose scree rather than stable snow. The easiest time to ascend is when there is sufficient snowpack to make consistent, on-snow travel possible.

From the Bunny Flat trailhead, hike about a mile to the Sierra Club hut at Horse Camp, site of a spring that is famous for the quality of its water—a good place to water-up. You'll also have a chance to try out the high-tech mulching toilet.

From here follow the Olberman Causeway, a raised stone trail built by J. M. "Mac" Olberman, first live-in caretaker of the hut. The causeway eventually gives way to a regular trail leading northwest. If you're getting an alpine start in the early-morning darkness, you may appreciate the arrows painted on the rocks, denoting switchbacks and turns. Higher on the route are rock cairns and wands to help you navigate. After a time the trail plateaus in the vicinity of Lake Helen. It's a very small lake and usually under snow, so the best indicators that you're at the lake may be the tents and the stone walls of bivouac shelters.

Above Lake Helen the climbing starts in earnest, and it's time to familiarize yourself with the Redbanks, the Thumb, and the Heart. The Redbanks is the prominent orange-red band of rock on the skyline above Avalanche Gully; the Thumb is the darker, rocky protuberance lower and to the right of the Redbanks. Most of the rockfall on the route comes from the Redbanks and from the Heart, a soft rock formation to the left (west) of the Redbanks. A helmet should be considered mandatory at this point, especially after dawn when the ice holding loose blocks of rock begins to soften.

The path of least resistance lies to the right of the Avalanche Gully proper. Aim for the saddle between the Redbanks and the Thumb. Most times of the year this will be a long snow climb requiring crampons and ice ax. In the fall, however, before the new snow, it can be a gravelly grovel.

Continue up, heading southeast of the Redbanks. Once you reach the saddle, continue into the Redbanks either through a short rock "chimney," or a bit of Class 3 face climbing, or up a tight snow couloir (gully) farther north. There is generally a trail in the scree and snow along the top of the Redbanks. Above this is a relatively flat spot with several rock-wall shelters that is a popular rest area. The switchbacked grade above here has earned the name Misery Hill. Atop Misery Hill rises a short snowfield and the final summit. A trail, snowpacked or sandy depending on time of year, leads to the top.

Descend by reversing the ascent route, watching carefully for rockfall below the Redbanks. Rockfall can be almost constant later in the day, after the sun loosens the matrix holding the rocks above.

2. CASTLE DOME

Highlights: A good warm-up before climbing Mount Shasta—or a good cool-down the day after a Shasta ascent. Surreal granitic terrain, where sharp cliffs alternate with rounded bulges. This climb is of an entirely different nature than those of the Shasta or Lassen volcanoes. The dome affords incredible views of Shasta and the surrounding country.
Distance: 6 miles round trip (only the last quarter-mile is not on a trail).
Difficulty: Class 3; moderate.
Trailhead Elevation: 2,750 feet
Summit Elevation: 4,700 feet
Elevation Gain: 1,950 feet
Best Months: May through October.
Maps: USGS Dunsmuir; DeLorme *Northern California Atlas and Gazetteer*, page 36.
Latitude: 41°10'52"N
Longitude: 112°23'19"W
Permits: No permit needed; $2.00 fee for entering the park.
Trailhead: Castle Crags State Park. Leave Interstate 5 at the Castle Crags/Castella exit (6 miles south of Dunsmuir and 49 miles north of Redding). Follow signs to Castle Crags State Park. Turn right just past the park headquarters and continue 1.5 miles through the campground and up a windy road to the trailhead. Follow the signs marking the Castle Dome Trail, which starts about 150 feet back down the road from the parking area.

You're probably in this part of California to climb Mount Shasta or Mount Lassen—or maybe you're a peak-bagger, heading south on Interstate 5, whose attention has been grabbed by the magnificent granite domes just west of the highway. In either case don't pass by Castle Dome, which stands in sharp contrast to the otherwise rolling volcanic terrain of the area. Castle Dome provides

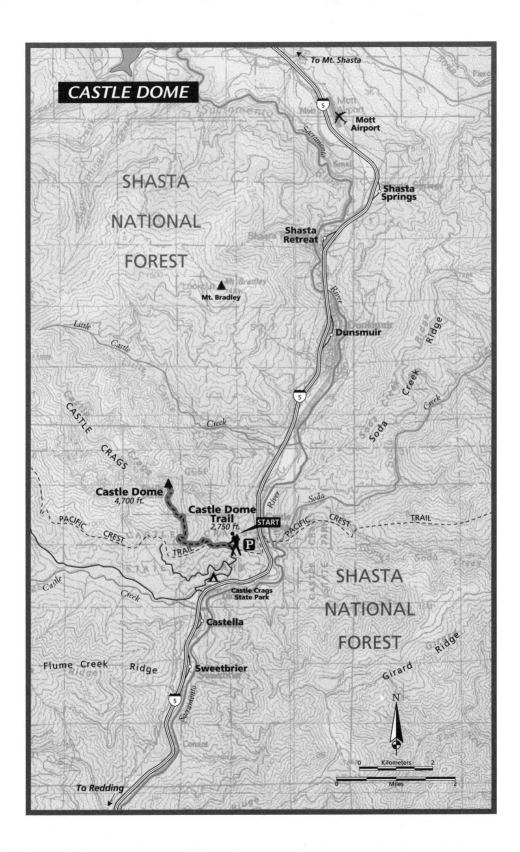

an enjoyable afternoon hike. If you're a rock climber, you'll find a wealth of seldom-climbed, classic granite in the area as well.

The Castle Dome Trail takes you first for about 2 miles through a low canopy of scrub oak forest. The trail then grants you your first complete view of the crags that gave the state park its name. The next half-mile or so travels through these rugged granite crags. Rock-climbing routes start right off the trail in various spots.

After a little over 2.5 miles you'll reach the base of Castle Dome proper. To travel this far is a worthwhile hike in itself, offering fine views of Mount Shasta and the surrounding crags, as well as idyllic picnic spots on granite slabs in the sun or under windswept pine trees.

For many hikers, however, the trip won't be complete without summiting the dome itself. The route from here is an exposed scramble on rounded granite. With careful routefinding the climb is fun, and relatively secure if you're careful. Find the major shoulder to the right of the center of the crag, and climb this to its high point. From there, a step across the major cleft in the rock leads to a couple of steep friction moves on the upper rock, the crux of the climb. Then traverse right and pick from any of the slab possibilities leading upward. The summit is wide and flat, and open to the world.

3. MOUNT LASSEN

Highlights: A relatively short (though steep) hike up a startlingly abrupt volcanic peak. The trail climbs out of scree and between small volcanic towers. As the highest mountain in the immediate area, it affords views of Mount Shasta and the surrounding area that are spectacular.

Distance: 5 miles round trip (all trail).

Difficulty: Class 2; moderate.

Trailhead Elevation: 8,453 feet

Summit Elevation: 10,457 feet

Elevation Gain: 2,004 feet

Best Months: July through October.

Maps: USGS Lassen Peak; DeLorme *Northern California Atlas and Gazetteer*, page 48.

Latitude: 40°29′16″N

Longitude: 121°30′14″W

Permits: Day use only, no permits required; fee for entrance to the park.

Trailhead: Lassen National Volcanic Park is about 50 miles east of Redding on Highway 44, and 50 miles east of Red Bluff on Highway 36. From either the south or north entrance to the park, follow signs to the Mount Lassen trailhead.

Mount Lassen is the southernmost peak of the Cascade Range, which runs from British Columbia through Washington and Oregon into Northern California. Start your ascent by the sign that indicates the Mount Lassen Trail, at the north

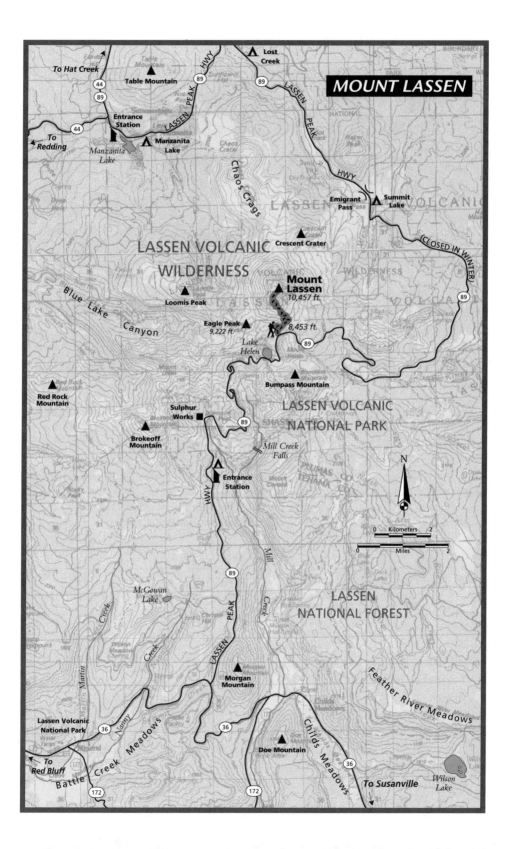

PHOTO: U.S. Geological Survey/Johnston, W. D. 213

Mount Lassen

side of the parking lot. The route is well traveled and easy to follow. Steep switch-backs cut between rock formations that suggest giant plastic chessmen left in the sun. The trail passes one false summit on its way to the top. The true high point will be obvious: The summit crater is a rare feature.

Interpretive signs and photos at the summit tell the story of Lassen's violent eruptions. Take time to walk the way around the crater and try to imagine the mountain as it once was. Mount Shasta can be seen to the northwest, the Sierra Nevada range to the south, and the Trinity Alps to the west.

4. EUREKA PEAK

Highlights: A prime representative of the transition peaks between the northern volcanoes and the Sierra range. At Eureka Peak, forested slopes give way to sheer andesite cliffs and blocks. The climb affords views from Lake Tahoe to Mount Lassen.

Distance: 6.6 miles round trip (all trail).

Difficulty: Class 2; moderate.

Trailhead Elevation: 5,500 feet

Summit Elevation: 7,497 feet

Elevation Gain: 1,997 feet

Best Months: May through October.

Maps: USGS Gold Lake; DeLorme *Northern California Atlas and Gazetteer*, page 70.

Latitude: 39°44'57"N

Longitude: 120°43'12"W

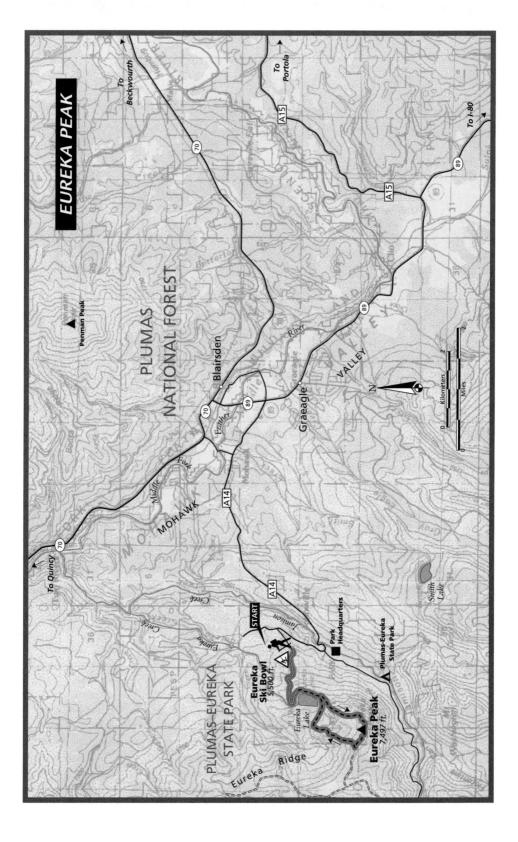

EUREKA PEAK

To Beckwourth

To Portola

A15

70

89

To I-80

A15

89

PLUMAS
NATIONAL FOREST

Penman Peak

Blairsden

River

70

89

VALLEY

89

N

Feather

Graeagle

2

2

Kilometers

Miles

0

0

Fork

Middle

A14

MOHAWK

To Quincy

70

Creek

A14

Smith
Lake

PLUMAS-EUREKA
STATE PARK

Eureka

Creek

START

Jamison

Park
Headquarters

Eureka
Ski Bowl
5,500 ft.

Plumas-Eureka
State Park

Eureka
Lake

Eureka Peak
7,497 ft.

Eureka Ridge

Eureka Peak

Permits: No permit needed; day use only.

Trailhead: From the intersection of Interstate 80 and Highway 89 at Truckee, head north on Highway 89 for about 52 miles to Graeagle. Here, turn west on County Road A14. Drive 5 miles, past the historic mining town of Johnsville, and up a steep grade to the end of the paved road, the parking area for what in winter is the Eureka Ski Bowl.

Eureka Peak is the sister summit of Sierra Buttes in the Plumas County mountains. The hike to the top of Eureka, though steep in spots, is short and largely shaded by pines, incense cedars, and oaks. From the trailhead, follow signs to Eureka Lake, a popular fishing spot. The trail to the lake is really a rocky access road used by the ski area. At times it skirts open meadow and at times switches back through manzanita-covered hillside. It's possible to drive to the lake with a vehicle of at least moderate clearance, cutting 2.5 miles from the round-trip distance to the summit.

Follow the lake along the dam side (north) to where the trail enters the woods. You'll soon reach a trail junction: Continue on the trail to the left, which goes along the ridge (the trail on the right will be part of your return loop). The trail becomes very steep for the next mile or so as it follows a ridgeline, still thankfully shaded. As the trail winds around to the south and ascends the summit plateau, the grade lessens and the taller trees give way to scrub oaks, manzanita, and convoluted rock formations. The summit is marked by a post on an obvious rocky loaf. A virtual tunnel through the dense brush allows access. From the summit, look north to see Mount Lassen and south to the Lake Tahoe peaks.

You can just reverse course for your descent. But for variety, make it a loop hike by following the trail past the summit for a half-mile or so, where it joins a fire road and trends slightly downhill. Then look for a marked split in the route: The left fork is the fire road and the right one is part of the trail that you passed earlier at the junction back near the lake. Follow this trail down a steep, wooded slope to the junction, where you'll rejoin the original route for the hike back to the trailhead.

5. SIERRA BUTTES

Highlights: Stark andesite towers and cliffs, nestled in snowfields much of the year. The trail is more exposed than that on Eureka Peak, often putting the hiker at the top or bottom of vertical tableaus. Rock climbing is popular in the area, including bolted routes on the summit block. The Sierra Buttes complex has the feel of the high mountains—looking like a peak from the Pacific Northwest transplanted to the northern Sierra foothills. There are spectacular views of Lake Tahoe, Mount Lassen, and Eureka Peak.

Distance: 5.2 miles round trip (all trail).

Difficulty: Class 2; easy/moderate.

Trailhead Elevation: 7,012 feet

Summit Elevation: 8,591 feet

Elevation Gain: 1,579 feet

Best Months: July through September.

Maps: USGS Sierra City; DeLorme *Northern California Atlas and Gazetteer*, page 70.

Latitude: 39°35′37″N

Longitude: 120°38′24″W

Permits: None needed for day use; wilderness permit required for overnight stay.

Trailhead: From the south, take Highway 49 east from Sierra City for about 5 miles to the Gold Lake turnoff at the Bassetts country store and turn left. Follow the Gold Lake–Lakes Basin road about a mile and a half to the Sardine Lake cutoff and go left. (From the north, take Highway 89 from Graeagle about 2 miles to the Gold Lake–Lakes Basin road and go south. Drive about 9 miles to the Sardine Lake cutoff and go right.) Now go 1.4 miles west up Sardine Lake Road to County Route S621; take this county route for 2.7 miles to its junction with Forest Road 93. Drive past Packer Lake and take the south fork for two-tenths of a mile to the trailhead, marked by a sign for Trail 12E06.

The Sierra Buttes climb offers a small summit with a handy fire lookout tower on the summit for taking in the 360-degree view. The andesite summit block is supported by dramatically uplifted rock.

From the trailhead, the hike (part of the Pacific Crest Trail) follows an old fire road up a steep grade through incense cedars and ponderosa pines. After a quarter-mile the fire road branches left; follow the trail that branches right. This trail

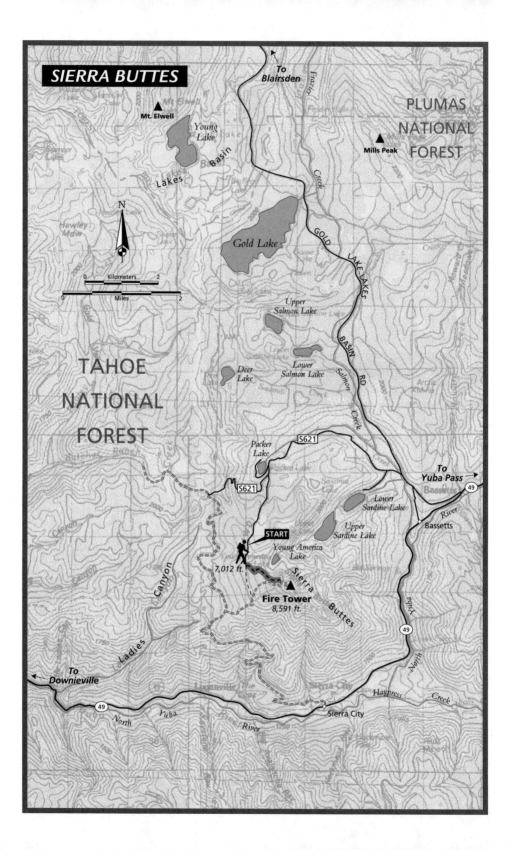

SIERRA BUTTES

PLUMAS NATIONAL FOREST

TAHOE NATIONAL FOREST

N

Kilometers 2

Miles 2

To Blairsden

Mt. Elwell

Young Lake

Mills Peak

Gold Lake

GOLD LAKE-LAKES BASIN RD

Upper Salmon Lake

Lower Salmon Lake

Deer Lake

Howley Mdw

Salmon Creek

Packer Lake

S621

S621

Lower Sardine Lake

Upper Sardine Lake

To Yuba Pass

49

Bassetts

START

Young America Lake

7,012 ft.

Sierra Buttes

Fire Tower
8,591 ft.

Canyon

Ladies

49

North Yuba River

To Downieville

Sierra City

49

Haypress Creek

North Yuba River

Sierra Buttes

travels through open manzanita, then bends around to follow south-southeast, affording views of Young America Lake and Upper and Lower Sardine Lakes.

From here the trail heads away from the ridge, toward the summit block. A jeep road from the south makes a trailhead along your route, about three-quarters of a mile from the summit. The trail now follows a rocky access road to the base of a metal stairway leading to the Sierra Buttes summit, with its fire lookout. The sporadically manned lookout tower building is locked when not in use, but the deck that surrounds it is open to the public. Rock climbers take note: There are many high-quality boulders in the vicinity.

Lake Tahoe Area

The Lake Tahoe area is a popular mountaineering destination. Situated at an elevation of 6,400 feet on the California–Nevada border, Lake Tahoe boasts cool summers, a welcome respite from the heat of California's Central Valley. Visitors arrive via Interstate 80 to the north and Highway 50 to the south. It's an easy place to get to. The peaks in the Tahoe area are lower than those of the greater Sierra Nevada, and the approach hikes are usually shorter.

The geological history of the formation of Lake Tahoe helps explain the diversity of the peaks in the area. Geological faulting and uplift exaggerated the local relief in the Tahoe valley, which sunk as its eastern side rose. Volcanic activity to the north sealed off the valley, giving it the opportunity to become a lake, filled with snowmelt, stream drainage, and glacial melt. The glaciers left their mark on some, but not all, of the peaks, resulting in a variety of mountain types that today provide a range of hiking experiences—from the angular, almost Martian landscape of Castle Peak to the clean granite topography of Freel Peak.

6. CASTLE PEAK

Highlights: A dramatic volcanic summit just north of Interstate 80 and west of Donner Summit, on the way to the high country from the Sacramento Valley—a worthwhile goal in itself, and also a good warm-up before tackling some of the other climbs in the Tahoe area. The view from Castle Peak includes most of the Tahoe peaks, Lake Tahoe, Sierra Buttes, Eureka Peak, and (on a clear day) Mount Lassen.
Distance: 5.4 miles round trip (all trail).
Difficulty: Class 2; easy/moderate.
Trailhead Elevation: 7,800 feet
Summit Elevation: 9,103 feet
Elevation Gain: 1,303 feet
Best Months: Early July through September.
Maps: USGS Norden; DeLorme *Northern California Atlas and Gazetteer*, page 81.
Latitude: 39°21'56"N
Longitude: 120°20'53"W
Trailhead: From Interstate 80, take the Castle Peak/Boreal Ridge exit (one exit west of the Donner Summit exit and one exit east of the Soda Springs exit). The trailhead is on the north side of the interstate, about a quarter-mile from the exit. There's a sign to Castle Peak, and a dirt parking area.

Castle Peak is the first significant mountain encountered along the drive to Lake Tahoe from the Sacramento Valley. It stands prominently north of the interstate, offering a moderate hike through varied terrain.

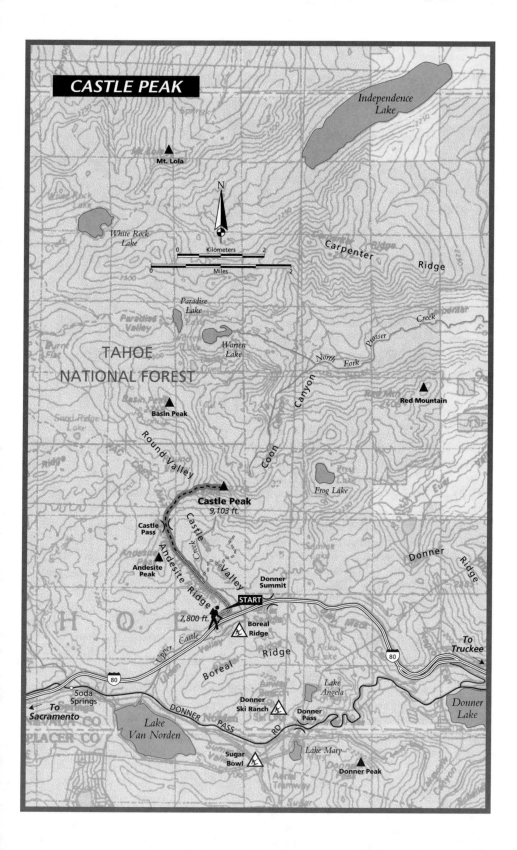

Castle Peak

The first part of the hiking route is along a dirt road. (You can drive another half-mile or so if you wish—and with a determined vehicle, especially with high clearance, you can cut close to a mile off the one-way distance.) The dirt road travels for the first half-mile under a canopy of Jeffery pines and incense cedars. When the road branches, stay left. The tree cover opens up, and the trail steepens. After walking for almost a mile, you'll reach a parking area for four-wheel-drive vehicles.

The trail now climbs steeply to Castle Pass and its junction with the Pacific Crest Trail. From the junction it's a little over a mile to the top of Castle Peak. Take the obvious trail branch along the ridge to the north-northeast. The trail is open, rocky, steep, and in some places exposed; the views are consequently panoramic and spectacular. Watch your footing.

7. PACIFIC CREST TRAIL TRAVERSE

From Donner Pass to Squaw Valley, including Donner Peak, Mount Judah, Mount Lincoln, Anderson Peak, and Tinker Knob

Highlights: A different sort of adventure from the other peaks in this book: a Pacific Crest Trail traverse from Donner Pass (Old Donner Summit) to Squaw Valley. An excellent trail run, (round trip is 50 kilometers if you exclude Donner Peak), this trail follows a ridge between the two end points, with five scramble summits along the way. The views include most of the Tahoe peaks, California's Central Valley to the west, and Nevada's basin and range country to the east. On a clear day you can see Mount Lassen.

Distance: 15.2 miles one way (all trail). From Donner Pass, cumulative mileages are: Donner Peak 1.9; Mount Judah 2.5; Mount Lincoln 3.8; Anderson Peak 6.3; Tinker Knob 7.2; Squaw Valley 15.2

Difficulty: Class 2; strenuous.

Trailhead Elevation: 7,060 feet

Summit Elevations: Donner Peak 8,019 feet; Mount Judah 8,243 feet; Mount Lincoln 8,383 feet; Anderson Peak 8,683 feet; Tinker Knob 8,949 feet.

Best Months: Early July through September, depending on snowpack.

Maps: USGS Norden; USGS Granite Chief; DeLorme *Northern California Atlas and Gazetteer*, page 81.

Permits: None needed for day use; wilderness permit required for overnight stay.

Trailhead: Donner Pass trailhead. From Interstate 80, take the Soda Springs exit if you're coming from the west, or the Donner Lake exit if you're coming from the east. In either case drive Highway 40 to Donner Pass (Old Donner Summit). The trailhead is just south of the highway on a small road that runs past the Alpine Skills International building. (When you drive past a strange-looking cantilevered building, you know you're going the right way.)

The trailhead for the Pacific Crest Trail has only limited parking, but there are plenty of places to park along the roads leading to it. (Do not, however, park in the Alpine Skills International lot.)

The trail first runs through a heavily wooded section. This part can be snow-bound early in the season, and overflows with vines, columbines, shooting stars, and heavy underbrush after the snow leaves. It can also be buggy. The trail rises out of this section to ascend switchbacks through granitic scree. This initial outcrop is part of the formation that makes up the Donner Summit rock-climbing area. After 1.25 miles you'll come to the north end of the Mount Judah loop trail. If Donner Peak and Mount Judah are among your objectives, turn left (east) onto this trail.

After about a quarter-mile along the loop trail, you'll come to an old dirt road heading east. Take this for half a mile or so to Donner Peak. Scramble up from the road to the granite cornices making up the summit block. Rock climbers find a lot of bouldering in this area, and short, bolted sport climbs as well. An easy route to the highest point lies to the left, winding along lower-angle sections of granite. The views are wide-ranging and dramatic.

Back on the loop trail it's about another three-quarters of a mile to the summit of Mount Judah. The trees thin out as you gain the ridge. Although Judah provides less a distinct summit than a high point along a ridge, the views from the top are nonetheless spectacular.

There is an interesting change in terrain here from granitic to volcanic. The plants known as mule ears grow along the open hillsides along the trail after this point. The large leaves that give the plant its name dry out in late summer. Once heard, the rustling sound of the breeze through these leaves is never forgotten, as distinctive as the cry of the peregrine falcon or call of the loon in a northern lake.

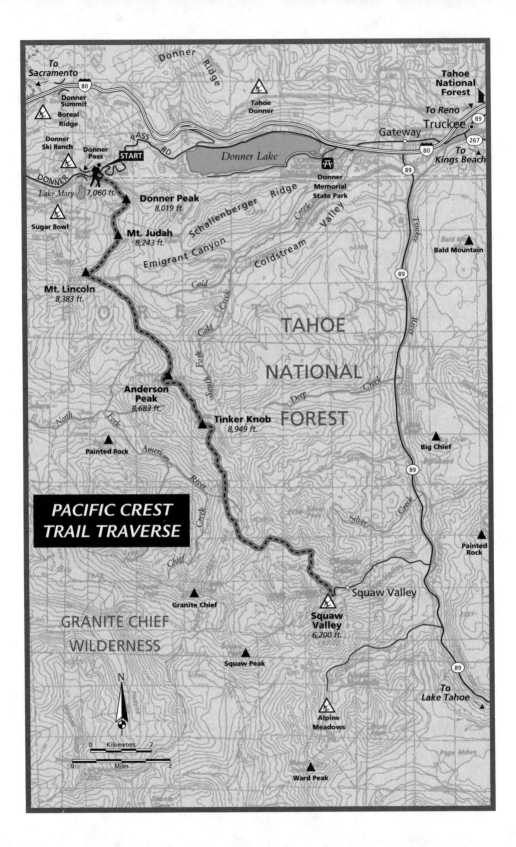

Follow the loop trail south, downhill, and back into the trees to the junction with the Pacific Crest Trail. Along the way is a spectacular view west of the Royal Gorge, a 4,000-foot cleft in the mountains that is largely unseen except from a few vantage points. After a short distance you will reach Roller Pass. From here it is a short, steep, tree-lined grade to a junction with a jeep trail that leads to the summit of Mount Lincoln, a short scramble above the trail.

After Mount Lincoln the trail drops into a long, open area. The route follows this ridge crest for the rest of the way to Anderson Peak and Tinker Knob; several miles of the trail to come are visible ahead. An 8,210-foot high point along the trail gives a good view of massive Anderson Peak.

As the trail approaches Anderson Peak, a small spur trail heads off to the left (east) to the Benson hut. Continue on the main trail, which runs to the west around Anderson Peak. At a short jog in the trail, a spur leads to the summit. The main trail, winding under the west face of Anderson, is composed of rocks that are irregular enough in shape that they provide a teetering, sometimes unstable surface. Watch your step. After passing the peak, the trail climbs back to the ridgeline.

South of Anderson Peak the trail keeps to the ridge for about 1.3 miles to Tinker Knob. The scrambling route to that summit is short and obvious. Tinker Knob marks the last of the peaks along this route. The most satisfying conclusion to this Pacific Crest Trail traverse is to continue on the 8 miles to Squaw Valley—but you could of course return the way you came for a round-trip hike of 14.4 miles.

To continue on to Squaw Valley, follow the Pacific Crest Trail for 4.2 miles through a granitic valley to the junction with the Granite Chief Trail. From here it is 3.8 miles to Squaw Valley. A heavily forested trail opens up more and more, granting views of the ski area and resort below. The trail ends behind the fire station, one block from the tram building and its parking.

8. MOUNT TALLAC

Highlights: The highest point close to Lake Tahoe. A reliable wildflower trail in June, the Mount Tallac hike goes through a variety of terrain, from forested to open meadows to dramatic andesite summit spikes. The views are spectacular, and sometimes you feel like you're looking straight down into Lake Tahoe's Emerald Bay. The summit is rocky, austere, and serene.

Distance: 10 miles round trip (last eighth of a mile is on rock with little discernible trail).

Difficulty: Class 2; strenuous.

Trailhead Elevation: 6,400 feet

Summit Elevation: 9,740 feet

Elevation Gain: 3,340 feet

Best Months: Early July through September, depending on snowpack.

Maps: USGS Emerald Bay; DeLorme *Northern California Atlas and Gazetteer*, page 89.

Latitude: 38°54′22″N

Fallen Leaf Lake and Lake Tahoe from Mount Tallac

Longitude: 120°05'52"W

Permits: None needed for day use; wilderness permit required for overnight stay.

Trailhead: From Highway 89 in South Lake Tahoe, the trailhead is 0.7 mile north of the Lake Tahoe Visitor's Information Center. Turn west at a sign to the Mount Tallac Trailhead. Follow this road for 0.3 mile, then turn left at the junction. The pavement ends 0.2 mile later. The trailhead is about half a mile beyond that point.

The ascent of Mount Tallac is an athletic undertaking. From the trailhead, start hiking up the old roadway. A dense canopy of Jeffrey pines and incense cedars shades the trail. Stay right at a trail junction after just a tenth of a mile. Mount Tallac looms in front of you.

From here the trail gets rockier and steeper and the forest opens up. Manzanita and wildflowers lead the way. The trail plateaus slightly after half a mile, then steepens again, warming you up for what lies ahead. In short order the trail follows a ridge crest, with Fallen Leaf Lake on the left and Mount Tallac on the right. The trail leaves the ridge at 1.2 miles and descends slightly, into white fir forest.

At 1.7 miles from the trailhead, you enter Desolation Wilderness and shortly thereafter reach Floating Island Lake. The trail here steepens through an open area that is filled with wildflowers in season. After a rise, featuring a view of Lake Tahoe, the trail drops down to cross Cathedral Creek. Above this is a trail junction (2.5 miles into the hike); go right, to Cathedral Lake.

After Cathedral Lake the trail becomes much steeper. The trees drop away and you ascend a rocky trail through a manzanita slope. The views, especially into the Desolation Wilderness, become increasingly panoramic. At 3.4 miles into the hike, stay left on the main trail at a junction. Another tenth of a mile

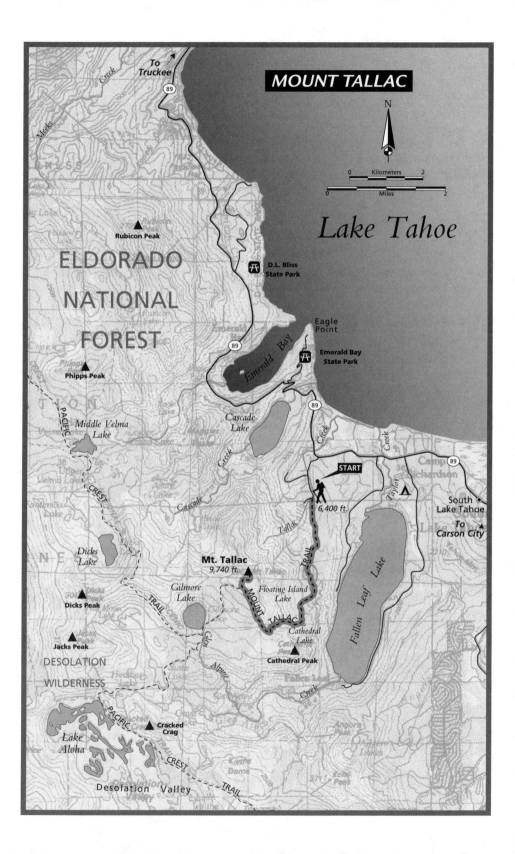

MOUNT TALLAC

N

Kilometers 2

Miles 2

Lake Tahoe

To Truckee

89

Meeks Creek

Rubicon Peak

ELDORADO

NATIONAL

FOREST

D.L. Bliss State Park

Eagle Point

89

Emerald Bay

Emerald Bay State Park

Phipps Peak

PACIFIC

CREST

Middle Velma Lake

Cascade Lake

Cascade Creek

89

START

6,400 ft.

Camp Richardson

89

South Lake Tahoe

To Carson City

Dicks Lake

Dicks Peak

TRAIL

Mt. Tallac
9,740 ft.

Gilmore Lake

Floating Island Lake

MOUNT TALLAC

TRAIL

Fallen Leaf Lake

Taylor Creek

Jacks Peak

DESOLATION

WILDERNESS

Glen

Alpine

Cathedral Lake

Cathedral Peak

PACIFIC

Cracked Crag

Lake Aloha

CREST

TRAIL

Desolation Valley

takes you to the top of the ridge, for a brief respite in steepness as you circle around the peak.

Another steep grade starts around mile 3.8. Wind-stunted, white-bark pines and wildflowers characterize this section of trail. At 4 miles you can see the summit. At a trail junction at mile 4.7, go right. At 4.9 miles, Lake Tahoe comes back into view. Various trails lead from here to the rocky summit just a tenth of a mile farther, where you can soak up the vistas of the Desolation Wilderness, Mount Ralston, Pyramid Peak, and the alpine lakes.

9. MOUNT ROSE

Highlights: The most prominent peak seen from Reno; also visible from all around the Tahoe basin. A desirable peak from aesthetics alone, it is complemented by a strenuous but pleasant hike through forest to windswept hillside and to volcanic austerity, up the third-highest peak in the Tahoe area. Mount Rose offers superb views, and wildflowers in season.

Distance: 12 miles round trip (all trail).

Difficulty: Class 2; strenuous.

Trailhead Elevation: 8,800 feet

Summit Elevation: 10,776 feet

Elevation Gain: 1,976 feet

Best Months: May through September.

Maps: USGS Mount Rose; DeLorme *Nevada Atlas and Gazetteer*, page 42.

Latitude: 39°25'54"N

Longitude: 119°54'58"W

Mount Rose

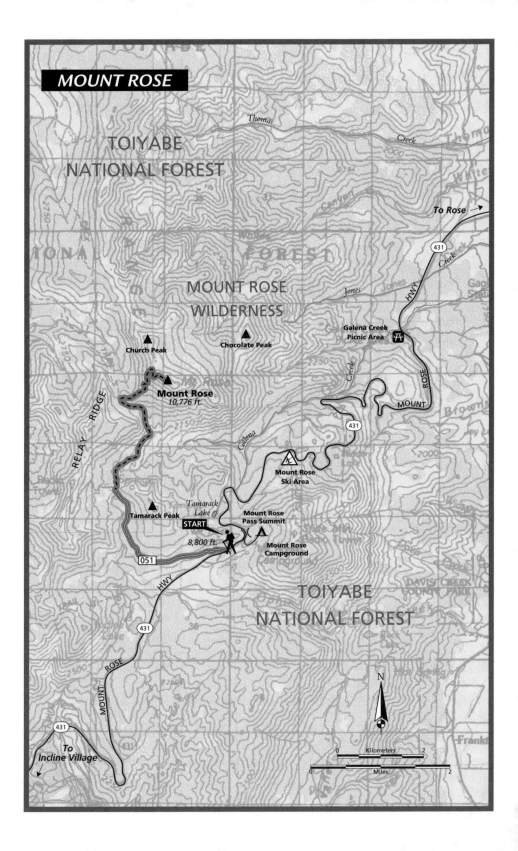

Permits: None needed for day use; wilderness permit required for overnight stay.
Trailhead: Drive south from Reno (for 10 miles) or north from Carson City
(for 19 miles) to the Mount Rose Highway (Highway 431). Drive west for about
10 miles to the trailhead, by a maintenance shed just west of the Mount Rose
Pass summit.

Mount Rose is in Nevada, but it's the third-highest peak in the Lake Tahoe basin,
which sits astride the California–Nevada border. Mount Rose has a striking
appearance when viewed from the east, and it offers a thoroughly enjoyable summit hike. Since the peak is only a few miles across the border from California, it
seemed to fit just fine in this book on California mountains.

The route follows a gravel road for the first 2.5 miles. At that point the trail
heads right and crosses Galena Creek. Follow the trail uphill through whitebark
pines to the border of the Mount Rose Wilderness Area at an open saddle. From
here the trail trends north and is open and steep. Switchbacks through lichen-
covered scree lead the last stretch to the summit. The summit register is in the
highest rock shelter, which offers a welcome break from the strong winds typical
of the summit.

10. FREEL PEAK

Highlights: The highest point of the Lake Tahoe area, with views into the basin
and range country in Nevada. A varied trail through both open and shaded
country, and less foot traffic than on Mount Tallac or Mount Rose, make this a
good day's choice. (You can combine this hike with an ascent of nearby Jobs
Sister and Jobs Peak for a three-summit day.)
Distance: 8 miles round trip (all trail).
Difficulty: Class 2; moderate/strenuous.
Trailhead Elevation: 8,420 feet
Summit Elevation: 10,881 feet
Elevation Gain: 2,461 feet
Best Months: Early July to October, depending on snowpack.
Maps: USGS Freel Peak; DeLorme *Northern California Atlas and Gazetteer*, page
90.
Latitude: 38°51'28"N
Longitude: 119°53'58"W
Permits: None needed for day use; wilderness permit required for overnight stay.
Trailhead: Take Highway 89 from South Lake Tahoe for 9.5 miles to Willow
Pass Road (Forest Road 051), 0.8 mile east of Luther Pass. Drive 2.6 miles up
Road 051 to a bridge across Willow Creek, then another 0.9 mile to a second
bridge. Just past this bridge, take a sharp left onto Forest Road 051F. Follow this
steep road, which crosses the creek again, for a few hundred yards and take the
right fork at a junction for 0.5 mile to the trailhead. (A high-clearance vehicle
may be necessary for this last section, and four-wheel drive is needed if the road
is wet.)

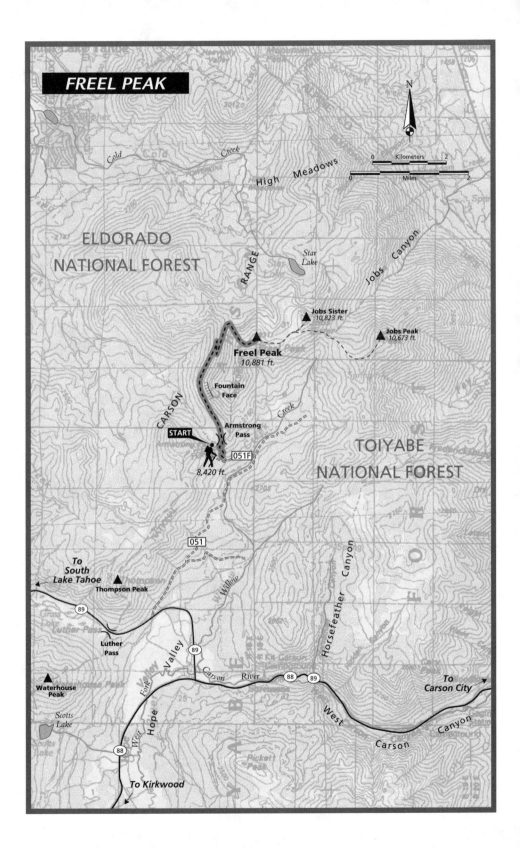

FREEL PEAK

ELDORADO
NATIONAL FOREST

TOIYABE
NATIONAL FOREST

N

Cold Creek
Cold
Cold Creek
High Meadows

Star Lake
RANGE
Jobs Canyon

Jobs Sister
10,823 ft.

Jobs Peak
10,673 ft.

Freel Peak
10,881 ft.

Fountain
Face

CARSON

Creek

Armstrong
Pass

START

051F

8,420 ft.

051

To
South
Lake Tahoe

Thompson Peak

Willow

Horsefeather Canyon

89

Luther
Pass

89

Waterhouse
Peak

West Fork Hope Valley

Valley

89

Carson River

88 89

To
Carson City

Scotts
Lake

West
Carson
Canyon

88

To Kirkwood

Picket Peak

0   Kilometers   2
0   Miles   2

Fountain Face, Freel Peak

Freel Peak offers a good hike to a scenic summit—along with the possibility of completing a triple-crown of Tahoe high points: Freel (10,881, highest of the Tahoe peaks); Jobs Sister (second-highest, at 10,823); and Jobs Peak (fourth-highest, at 10,673).

From the trailhead, begin the steep, half-mile grade to Armstrong Pass, where the route joins the Tahoe Rim Trail. The trail then goes north about 1.3 miles to Fountain Face. The trail skirts this formation for about a quarter-mile or so, and there are several established rock-climbing routes as well as new route opportunities. The rock is ample and abundant, but often abrasive and friable. This is adventure climbing.

From Fountain Face the trail steepens, trending slightly east of north until you reach a major switchback. After 3.5 miles from the trailhead, a junction with the smaller trail to Freel Peak is reached. This junction, a rocky saddle at 9,730 feet, is the high point of the Tahoe Rim Trail.

The path now switchbacks up a loose, extremely steep trail through scrub brush. After about half a mile the grade, though still steep, eases. The obvious trail winds up an open talus field to the top for a panoramic view only slightly marred by the summit radio antenna.

From the summit you'll get a good look at Freel's neighbors to the east: Jobs Sister and Jobs Peak. You can now return the way you came, or continue on to these other two peaks. If you take on all three peaks, you'll rack up about 13 miles total for the day.

Freel Peak (center) with Jobs Sister and Jobs Peak (right) as seen from Mount Tallac

11. JOBS PEAK

Highlights: Secluded location, offering views of the basin and range country in Nevada while still being close to Lake Tahoe. (This climb can be combined the same day with ascents of neighboring Freel Peak and Jobs Sister; see Freel Peak, climb #10.)

Distance: 12 miles round trip (all trail).

Difficulty: Class 2; strenuous.

Trailhead Elevation: 8,420 feet

Summit Elevation: 10,673 feet

Elevation Gain: 2,253 feet

Best Months: Early July through September.

Maps: USGS Woodfords; DeLorme *Northern California Atlas and Gazetteer*, page 90.

Latitude: 38°51'45"N

Longitude: 119°51'38"W

Permits: None needed for day use; wilderness permit required for overnight stay.

Trailhead: See Freel Peak, climb #10; same trailhead.

The climb of Jobs Peak first follows the 4-mile-long trail to the summit of Freel Peak. From Freel Peak, follow the obvious ridgeline toward nearby Jobs Sister for half a mile. At that point, halfway between Freel and Jobs Sister, simply hike due east, dropping 500 to 600 feet in elevation to a saddle between Jobs Sister and Jobs Peak. Then hike the ridge to the Jobs Peak summit.

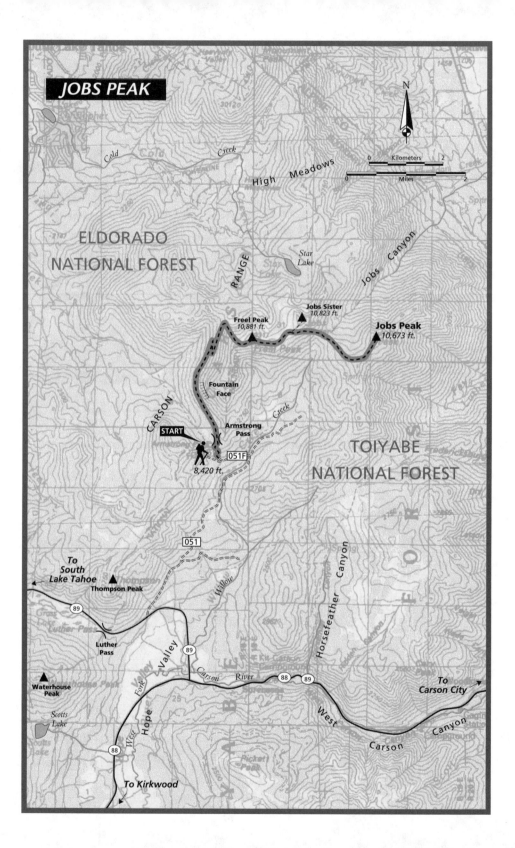

JOBS PEAK

N

ELDORADO
NATIONAL FOREST

High Meadows

Cold Creek

Star Lake

Jobs Canyon

RANGE

Jobs Sister
10,823 ft.

Freel Peak
10,881 ft.

Jobs Peak
▲ 10,673 ft.

Fountain
Face

Creek

CARSON

Armstrong
Pass

START

051F

TOIYABE
NATIONAL FOREST

8,420 ft.

051

To
South
Lake Tahoe

Thompson Peak
▲

Horsefeather Canyon

89

Willow

Luther
Pass

89

Carson River

88

89

To
Carson City

Waterhouse
Peak
▲

West Hope Valley

West

Carson

Canyon

Scotts
Lake

88

To Kirkwood

0   Kilometers   2
0   Miles   2

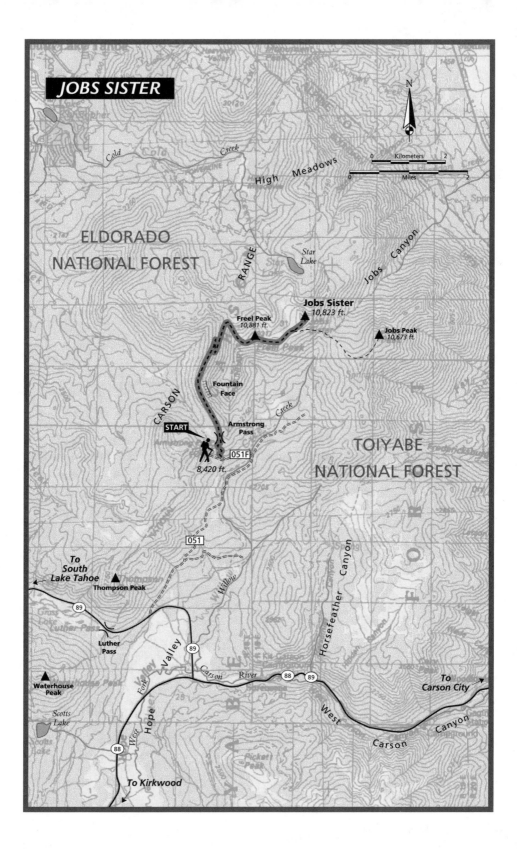

JOBS SISTER

ELDORADO
NATIONAL FOREST

TOIYABE
NATIONAL FOREST

High Meadows

Cold   Cold   Creek

RANGE

Star
Lake

Jobs   Canyon

Freel Peak
10,881 ft.

Jobs Sister
10,823 ft.

Jobs Peak
10,673 ft.

CARSON

Fountain
Face

Creek

Armstrong
Pass

START

051F

8,420 ft.

051

To
South
Lake Tahoe

Thompson Peak

Willow

Horsefeather Canyon

89

Luther
Pass

89

Valley

Fork

Carson   River

88   89

To
Carson City

Waterhouse
Peak

West   Hope

West

Carson   Canyon

Scotts
Lake

88

To Kirkwood

Kilometers

Miles

Since you've reached two summits already on this outing, you might as well add a third. The summit of Jobs Sister is easily reached via the ridge between it and Freel Peak. Total round-trip mileage for all three summits: about 13.

12. JOBS SISTER

Highlights: The second-highest peak in the Tahoe area, with views of the basin and range country in Nevada. (This climb can be combined the same day with ascents of neighboring Freel Peak and Jobs Peak; see Freel Peak, climb #10.)

Distance: 10 miles round trip (all trail).

Difficulty: Class 2; strenuous.

Trailhead Elevation: 8,420 feet

Summit Elevation: 10,823 feet

Elevation Gain: 2,403 feet

Best Months: Early July to October, depending on snowpack.

Maps: USGS Freel Peak; DeLorme *Northern California Atlas and Gazetteer*, page 90.

Latitude: 38°51'45"N

Longitude: 119°53'01"W

Permits: None needed for day use; wilderness permit required for overnight stay.

Trailhead: See Freel Peak, climb #10; same trailhead.

Jobs Sister is an irresistible side trip from the summit of Freel Peak. Just follow the obvious ridgeline for 1 mile to the east-northeast. You'll feel on top of the world hiking this scenic crest at 10,500 feet. The eastern views are even better than those from Freel Peak.

Yosemite National Park

Yosemite, one of the first national parks, was established October 1, 1890. From foothills to mountains topping 13,000 feet in elevation, from digger pines and bay laurels to stands of giant Sequoia, Yosemite has a wide diversity of terrain, elevation, and biological zones.

Our tour of the Yosemite area approaches from the northern boundary, with Matterhorn Peak, and moves down to Mount Conness before entering the Tuolumne high country at 9,900-foot Tioga Pass, the eastern entrance to the park. The first stop here is Mount Dana, right at the entrance. From here we go to the Tuolumne backcountry peaks of Amelia Earhart, Mount Lyell, and Mount Maclure. After that we visit Cathedral Peak above Tuolumne Meadows. The Clouds Rest hike gets us from Tuolumne down into Yosemite Valley proper. And from the valley, what better way to end the tour than with a hike up the dramatic cable route to the top of Half Dome.

13. MATTERHORN PEAK (SOUTHEAST SLOPE/EAST COULOIR)

Highlights: Aesthetically pleasing: From the trailhead, from the town of Bridgeport, or from Highway 395 and beyond, it commands the eye. You will know which one it is and why you want to climb it. Matterhorn is the northernmost major peak of the High Sierra, with spectacular views from the summit.

Distance: 8 miles (round trip or loop); all trail for the Horse Creek Pass round trip; the East Couloir loop option involves almost 2 miles of off-trail hiking.

Difficulty: Class 2; moderate/strenuous

Trailhead Elevation: 7,092 feet

Summit Elevation: 12,279 feet

Elevation Gain: 5,187 feet

Best Months: June through September.

Maps: USGS Matterhorn Peak; DeLorme *Northern California Atlas and Gazetteer*, page 101; National Geographic, Yosemite National Park.

Latitude: 38°05'34"N

Longitude: 119°22'49"W

Permits: None needed for day use; wilderness permit required for overnight stay.

Trailhead: The Twin Lakes trailhead is along the shore of the western Twin Lake in the resort community of Mono Village, 15 miles west of Bridgeport, California, at the terminus of the Twin Lakes road.

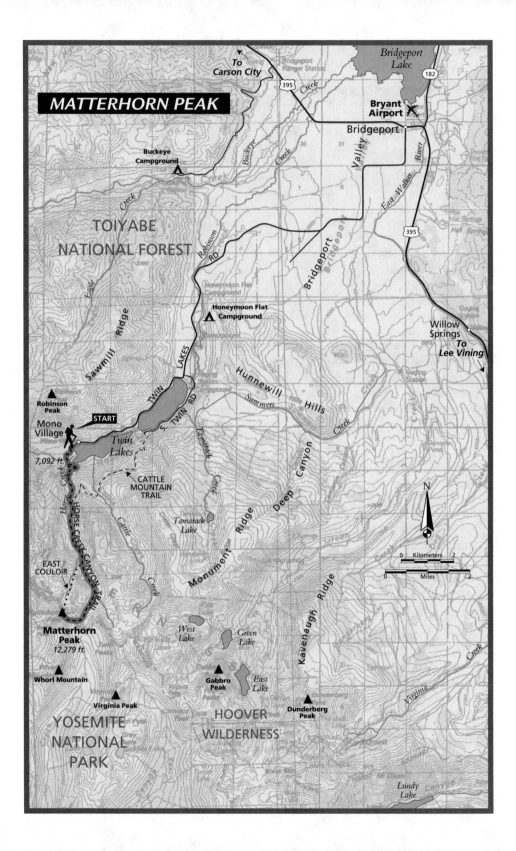

Matterhorn Peak

Matterhorn Peak sits in the northeastern corner of Yosemite, with the national park boundary running right across its summit. Though only 4 miles from trailhead to summit, the elevation gain is over 5,000 feet, pushing what would be a moderate climb into the strenuous category. For all this, the climb is mostly straightforward and follows well-used trails the whole way.

From the trailhead at Twin Lakes, follow the Horse Creek Canyon Trail 3.5 miles up switchbacks to Horse Creek Pass. In early season there will be snow; later in the year you'll encounter some minor creek crossings. Any time of year, the clear sound of flowing water will be a constant companion all the way to the pass. From the pass, the nature of the ascent changes: The wooded path gives way to a use trail through boulders and a gravelly hillside to the final rocky summit.

To descend, either reverse the ascent route or descend the obvious East Couloir (east gully) for a loop return. This option demands more technical ability than the ascent route does, especially if the couloir is snow-filled—but it's a practical alternative descent route for those with some climbing experience. Keep your wits about you and it is an easy variant. Cross the creek and rejoin the ascent trail at a point about 2.5 miles from the trailhead.

14. MOUNT CONNESS

Highlights: A challenging, classic Sierra ascent, with varied terrain and great views of the High Sierra, the Conness Glacier, and Saddlebag Lake. This hike starts high and is largely above tree line. The meadows and creek crossing in the beginning give way to open vistas of granitic terrain.

Distance: 10.4 miles round trip (almost all trail except for a short portion of Class 3 scrambling on the pass between Mount Conness and White Mountain).

Mount Conness

Difficulty: Class 3; strenuous
Trailhead Elevation: 10,000 feet
Summit Elevation: 12,590 feet
Elevation Gain: 2,590 feet
Best Months: June through September.
Maps: USGS Tioga Pass; DeLorme *Northern California Atlas and Gazetteer*, page 111; National Geographic, Yosemite National Park.
Latitude: 37°58'02"N
Longitude: 119°19'09"W
Permits: None needed for day use; wilderness permit required for overnight stay.
Trailhead: Saddlebag Lake. From Highway 120 at a point 4 miles east of Tioga Pass and 13 miles west of Lee Vining, take the Saddlebag Lake Road leading north. The trailhead is at Sawmill walk-in campground just south of Saddlebag Lake. It is also possible to start from the south end of Saddlebag Lake itself.

Mount Conness is a popular peak with rock climbers because of its famous Harding Route, one of the great Sierra wall climbs. The route described here is nontechnical, however, but spectacular and challenging—it feels longer than it looks on the map.

From the trailhead, walk west through the campground and through the Carnegie Institute experimental station. The trail winds through open meadow and makes some creek crossing that will wake you up in early season. From here, follow the trail to the pass between Mount Conness and White Mountain, above Alpine Lake. The pass, at 11,400 feet, is the crux of the climb. The pass is often

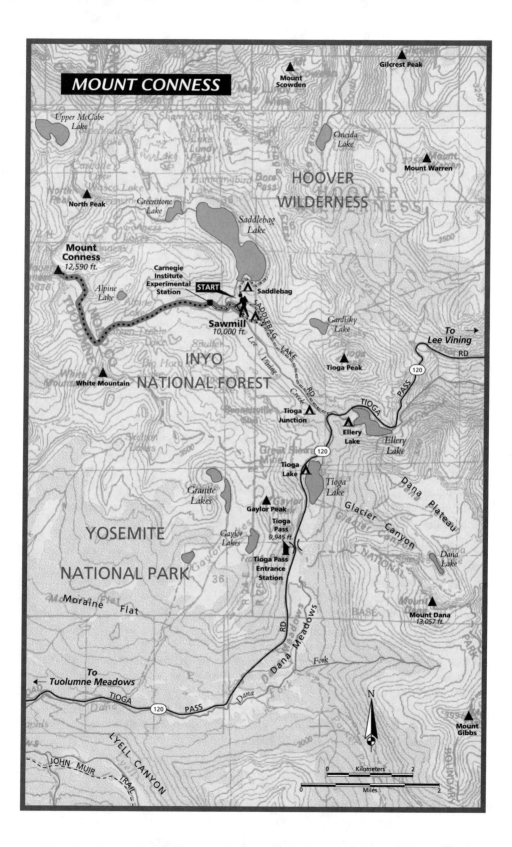

snow-filled, and it tends to be icy and hazardous early in the morning, before softening as the day warms up. Pick your way through the line of least resistance via Class 3 scrambling.

Beyond the pass, head northwest up the broad plateau toward the summit. As a side trip, look over the cliff on the left margin of the plateau for a view of the southwest face and its technical Harding Route to the summit. Back on your route, an old surveyor's trail threads around blocks to the top.

15. MOUNT DANA

Highlights: The second-highest peak in Yosemite; perched on the very eastern edge of Yosemite and the Sierra. Mount Dana is an accessible High Sierra peak of only moderate difficulty. You'll find incredible wildflowers, in season, on this aesthetic hike largely through open, rocky terrain. Views from the summit highlight the dramatic contrasts between the mountains and the basin-and-range province of Nevada. Another reward is the optional glissading on the descent for all skill levels.
Distance: 5.8 miles round trip (all trail).
Difficulty: Class 2; moderate.
Trailhead Elevation: 9,990 feet
Summit Elevation: 13,057 feet
Elevation Gain: 3,067 feet
Best Months: June through September.
Maps: USGS Mount Dana; DeLorme *Northern California Atlas and Gazetteer*, page 111; National Geographic, Yosemite National Park.
Latitude: 37°53'59"N
Longitude: 119°13'13"W
Permits: None needed for day use; wilderness permit required for overnight stay. Entrance fee charged to enter Yosemite National Park.
Trailhead: Tioga Pass entrance kiosk, where you pay the entrance fee as you enter the park from the east.

Standing watch over Tioga Pass, Mount Dana is a gateway to Yosemite and the Sierra. The unmarked trail starts at the Tioga Pass entrance kiosk. There are rest rooms and parking just west of the kiosk.

The trail starts as a moderate uphill route through Dana Meadows. From this point until the rocky heights farther up the trail, there's often a visual cacophony of wildflowers: lupine, Indian paintbrush, phlox, cow parsnip, columbine, cinquefoil, and more. They're likely to be most vibrant in July, right after the snowmelt.

Beyond the meadows the trail steepens. After a series of switchbacks, the trail becomes rocky, with little plant life after you've reached an elevation of about 11,000 feet. A bit farther, the trail plateaus on a rocky shoulder, with a giant cairn, at 11,500 feet.

Continue up and left toward the skyline ridge on what starts out as a fairly well-defined trail but soon becomes rather indefinite. A number of small trails all lead to the summit; generally keep near the ridgeline. From the summit, you look

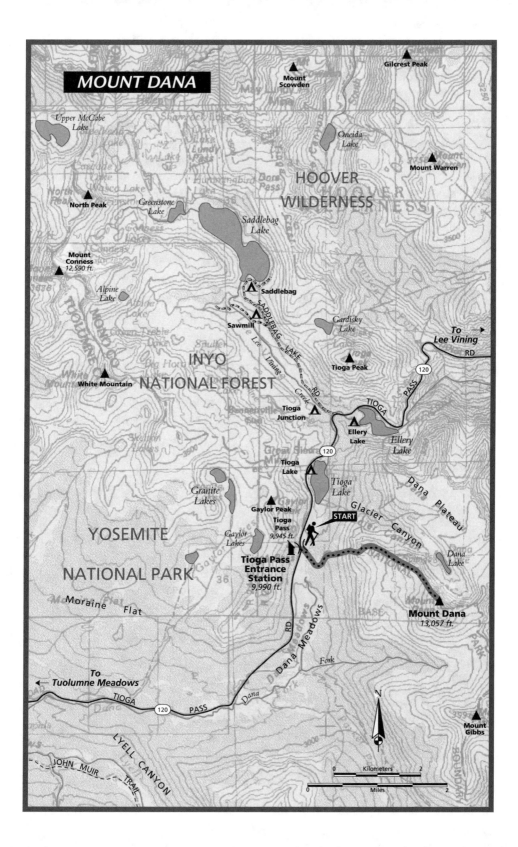

MOUNT DANA

Gilcrest Peak

Mount Scowden

Upper McCabe Lake

Oneida Lake

HOOVER WILDERNESS

Mount Warren

North Peak

Greenstone Lake

Saddlebag Lake

Mount Conness 12,590 ft.

Alpine Lake

Saddlebag

Sawmill

Gardisky Lake

To Lee Vining RD

INYO NATIONAL FOREST

Tioga Peak

White Mountain

120

TIOGA PASS

Tioga Junction

Ellery Lake

Ellery Lake

Dana Plateau

120

Tioga Lake

Granite Lakes

Gaylor Peak

Tioga Lake

YOSEMITE

Gaylor Lakes

Tioga Pass 9,945 ft.

START

Glacier Canyon

Dana Lake

NATIONAL PARK

Tioga Pass Entrance Station 9,990 ft.

Mount Dana 13,057 ft.

Moraine Flat

D Dana Meadows

To Tuolumne Meadows

Fork

N

TIOGA PASS

120

Dana

Fork

Mount Gibbs

LYELL CANYON

JOHN MUIR TRAIL

0   Kilometers   2

0   Miles   2

almost straight down 9,000 feet to Mono Lake. Watch for white pelicans making their way from Mono Lake to points west.

16. AMELIA EARHART PEAK (NORTHEAST RIDGE)

Highlights: An underappreciated gem of the Tuolumne backcountry. An easy and rewarding scramble puts you on top of this peak that rises to nearly 12,000 feet.

Distance: 14 miles round trip (12 miles on trail, 2 miles off trail).

Difficulty: Class 2; moderate.

Trailhead Elevation: 8,750 feet

Summit Elevation: 11,974 feet

Elevation Gain: 3,224 feet

Best Months: June through October.

Maps: USGS Vogelsang Peak; DeLorme *Northern California Atlas and Gazetteer*, page 111; National Geographic, Yosemite National Park.

Latitude: 37°47′09″N

Longitude: 119°17′94″W

Permits: None needed for day use; wilderness permit required for overnight stay. Entrance fee charged to enter Yosemite National Park.

Trailhead: Tuolumne Meadows trailhead (just before Tuolumne Lodge).

Popular with trail runners, Amelia Earhart Peak is also a satisfying day hike from Tuolumne. It can also be a warm-up on an overnight approach to Mounts Lyell and Maclure. For the truly, shall we say, inspired, a one-day ascent of all three peaks is an ultramarathon epic.

Amelia Earhart Peak

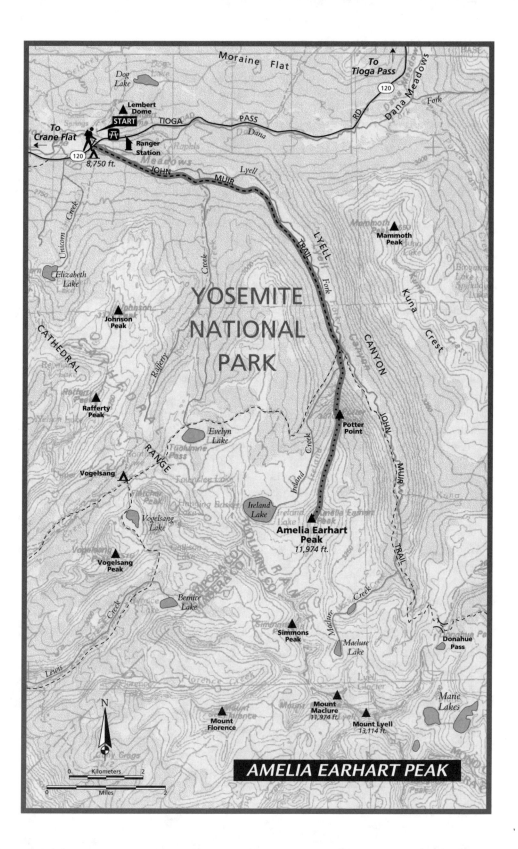

AMELIA EARHART PEAK

To ascend Earhart Peak, start at the Tuolumne Meadows trailhead and take the John Muir Trail down Lyell Canyon and along the Lyell Fork of the Tuolumne River. After 5.5 miles, Potter Point appears on your right; follow its ridge up scree and blocks to the summit. Reverse your route to descend.

17. MOUNT LYELL (EAST ARÊTE)

Highlights: The highest peak in Yosemite National Park. Mount Lyell dominates the Tuolumne high country. With its summit spire extending out of the glacier, it would be a desirable peak anywhere. Add its serene, remote location, and it becomes a sought-after and rewarding adventure.

Distance: 24 miles round trip (22 miles on trail; 2 miles off trail).

Difficulty: Class 3; very strenuous; bring ice ax.

Trailhead Elevation: 8,750 feet

Summit Elevation: 13,114 feet

Elevation Gain: 4,364 feet

Best Months: June through September.

Maps: USGS Mount Lyell; DeLorme *Northern California Atlas and Gazetteer*, page 111; National Geographic, Yosemite National Park.

Latitude: 37°44'24"N

Longitude: 119°16'16"W

Permits: None needed for day use; wilderness permit required for overnight stay. Entrance fee charged to enter Yosemite National Park.

Trailhead: Tuolumne Meadows trailhead (just before Tuolumne Lodge).

Mount Lyell as seen from the Lyell Fork of the Toulumne River

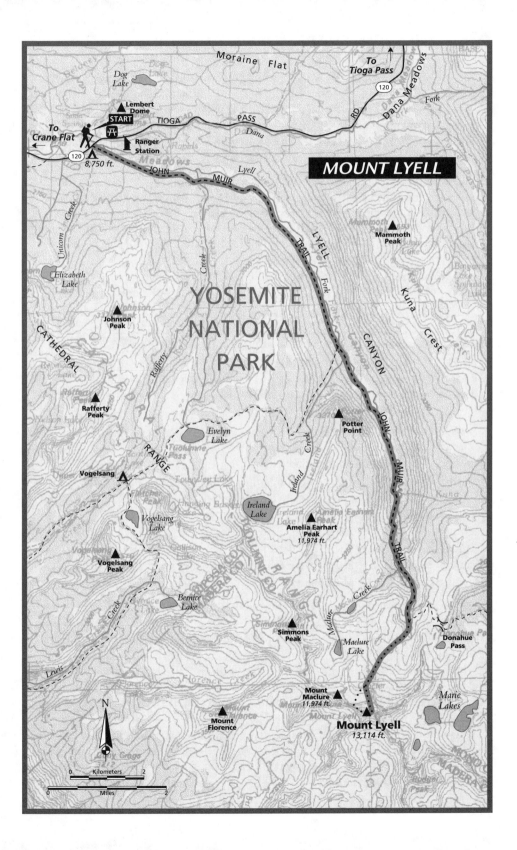

Moraine Flat

Dog Lake

To Tioga Pass

120

Dana Meadows

RD

Fork

Lembert Dome

START

Ranger Station

TIOGA PASS

Dana

120

To Crane Flat

8,750 ft.

JOHN

Rapids

MUIR

Meadows

Lyell

MOUNT LYELL

LYELL

TRAIL

Fork

Mammoth Peak

Mammoth

Unicorn

Creek

Kuna Crest

Elizabeth Lake

YOSEMITE NATIONAL PARK

Creek

Johnson

Johnson Peak

CANYON

Rafferty

Rafferty Peak

Evelyn Lake

Potter Point

JOHN

RANGE

CATHEDRAL

Ireland

Creek

Vogelsang

Vogelsang Lake

Ireland Lake

Amelia Earhart Peak

MUIR

Vogelsang Peak

Amelia Earhart Peak
11,974 ft.

Bernice Lake

TRAIL

Creek

Lewis

Creek

Maclure

Creek

Simmons Peak

Maclure Lake

Donahue Pass

Florence Creek

Mount Florence

Mount Maclure
11,974 ft.

Mount Lyell
13,114 ft.

Marie Lakes

N

Kilometers
0   2

Miles
0   2

Mount Lyell is a massive peak surrounded by snow and glaciers, rising beside its impressive neighbor, Mount Maclure. This is a long hike, so plan accordingly. Most parties will bivouac along the way and do this climb in two or even three days from the trailhead (though it is often done in one long day). Check at the Tuolumne ranger station (where you get your wilderness permit) for information on the sites along the way that are available for camping.

From the Tuolumne Meadows trailhead, take the John Muir Trail down Lyell Canyon, along the Lyell Fork of the Tuolumne River. Before Donohue Pass, leave the trail and scramble up slabs toward Lyell Glacier. Cross the glacier (no crevasses) and aim for the col (high pass) east of the main summit, passing to the right of a large rocky ridge in the middle of the glacier. From the col, follow the east *arête* (ridge) to the summit.

For the descent, drop west to another high pass—the col between Lyell and Maclure—and descend the glacier to slabs leading back to the John Muir Trail.

18. MOUNT MACLURE (SOUTHEAST RIDGE)

Highlights: A companion peak to Mount Lyell; if you liked Lyell, there is more to keep the adventure going. Great western views.
Distance: 25 miles round trip (21 miles on trail, 4 miles off trail).
Difficulty: Class 3; strenuous; bring ice ax.
Trailhead Elevation: 8,750 feet
Summit Elevation: 11,974 feet
Elevation Gain: 3,224 feet
Best Months: June through September.
Maps: USGS Mount Lyell; DeLorme *Northern California Atlas and Gazetteer*, page 111; National Geographic, Yosemite National Park.
Latitude: 37°44'24"N
Longitude: 119°16'16"W
Permits: None needed for day use; wilderness permit required for overnight stay. Entrance fee charged to enter Yosemite National Park.
Trailhead: Tuolumne Meadows trailhead (just before Tuolumne Lodge).

The trek to Mount Maclure travels the same route as that to neighboring Mount Lyell, making it very tempting to climb both peaks in the same trip. From the Tuolumne Meadows trailhead, take the John Muir Trail down Lyell Canyon, along the Lyell Fork of the Tuolumne River.

To reach the Maclure summit, leave the main trail before Donohue Pass and scramble up slabs toward Lyell Glacier. Aim for the right (west margin) of the glacier and head directly to the col (high pass) between Lyell and Maclure. From the col, follow the ledges west to the top of Maclure.

If you want to climb both peaks, first ascend Lyell (see Mount Lyell, climb #17). Then descend west to the Lyell-Maclure Col. Assess your physical state and decide if you really have enough gas for the second ascent. Ascend ledges and talus to the Maclure summit.

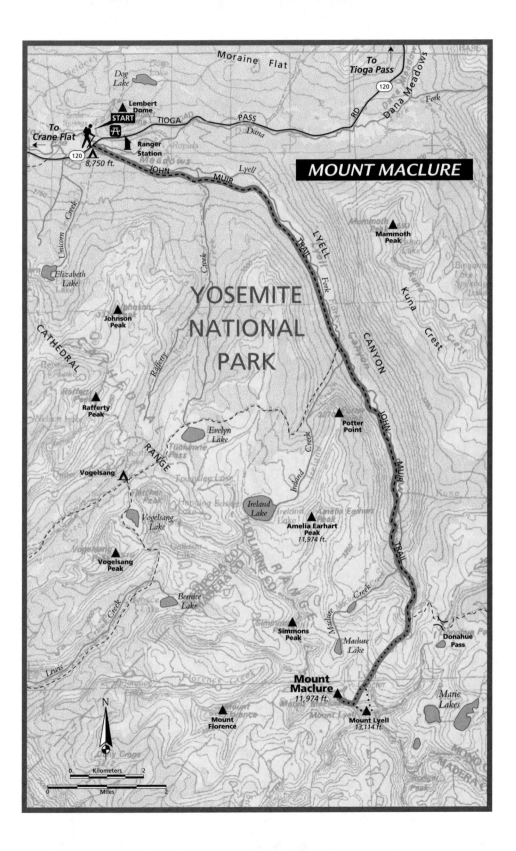

MOUNT MACLURE

YOSEMITE
NATIONAL
PARK

Moraine Flat

To
Tioga Pass

120

Dog Lake

Dog
Lake

Lembert
Dome

START

TIOGA   PASS

Dana

RD

Dana Meadows

Fork

To
Crane Flat

120

Ranger
Station

8,750 ft.

Rapids

Meadows

JOHN

MUIR

Lyell

TRAIL

Lyell

Fork

LYELL

Mammoth

Mammoth
Peak

Kuna

Crest

Unicorn

Creek

Elizabeth
Lake

CATHEDRAL

Johnson

Johnson
Peak

Creek

Rafferty

CANYON

JOHN

Kuna

Rafferty
Peak

Evelyn
Lake

Potter
Point

MUIR

RANGE

Tuolumne Pass

Townsley Lake

Creek

Ireland

TRAIL

Vogelsang

Vogelsang
Lake

Ireland
Lake

Ireland Lake

Amelia Earhart

Amelia Earhart
Peak
11,974 ft.

King

Vogelsang
Peak

Gallison

Bernice
Lake

Creek

Simmons

Simmons
Peak

Maclure

Creek

Maclure
Lake

Donahue
Pass

Lewis

Creek

Florence Creek

Mount
Florence

Mount
Florence

Mount Maclure

Mount
Maclure
11,974 ft.

Mount Lyell

Mount Lyell
13,114 ft.

Marie
Lakes

N

Kilometers   2

Miles   2

Photo: U.S. Geological Survey/Gilbert, G. K. 2104

Mount Maclure (right) and Mount Lyell (left)

To descend Maclure, drop back to the Lyell–Maclure Col and head down the glacier to the slabs leading back to the John Muir Trail.

19. CATHEDRAL PEAK

Highlights: One of the classics of Tuolumne and the High Sierra. Cathedral Peak is a striking formation, seen from many places throughout Yosemite. It offers a reasonably short hike to a technically interesting peak. The summit affords great views of the Tuolumne dome country.

Distance: 6 miles round trip (4.5 miles on trail, 1.5 miles off trail).

Difficulty: Class 4; moderate.

Trailhead Elevation: 8,700 feet

Summit Elevation: 10,911 feet

Elevation Gain: 2,211 feet

Best Months: June through September.

Maps: USGS Tenaya Lake; DeLorme *Northern California Atlas and Gazetteer*, page 111; National Geographic, Yosemite National Park.

Latitude: 37°50′50″N

Longitude: 119°24′18″W

Permits: None needed for day use; wilderness permit required for overnight stay. Entrance fee charged to enter Yosemite National Park.

Trailhead: Cathedral Peak Trailhead, 1 mile west of the Tuolumne Meadows store.

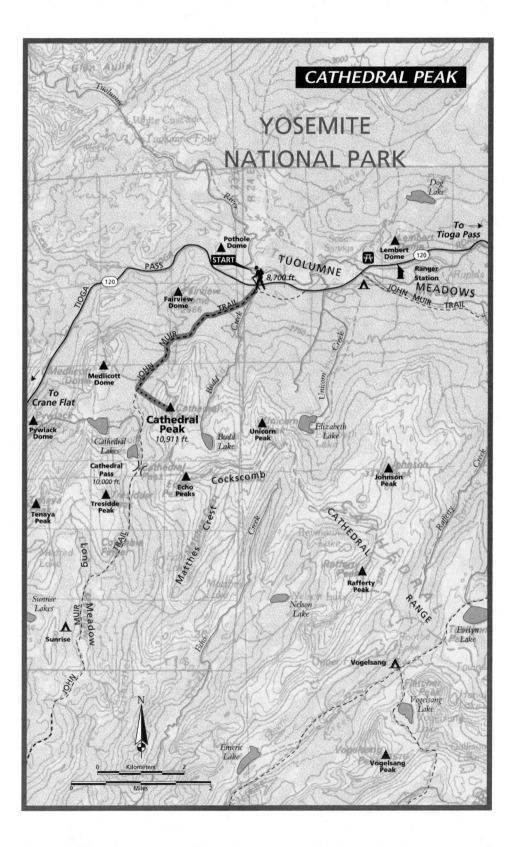

CATHEDRAL PEAK

YOSEMITE
NATIONAL PARK

To
Tioga Pass

Dog
Lake

Pothole
Dome

START

TUOLUMNE

Lembert
Dome

Ranger
Station

MEADOWS

8,700 ft.

PASS

Fairview
Dome

JOHN MUIR TRAIL

TIOGA

120

TRAIL

Budd

Creek

Unicorn Creek

Medlicott
Dome

JOHN MUIR

To
Crane Flat

Pywiack
Dome

**Cathedral
Peak**
10,911 ft.

Budd
Lake

Unicorn
Peak

Elizabeth
Lake

Johnson
Peak

Cathedral
Lakes

Cathedral
Pass
10,000 ft.

Echo
Peaks

Cockscomb

Creek

Tenaya
Peak

Tresidde
Peak

TRAIL

Matthes Crest

Rafferty

CATHEDRAL

Rafferty
Peak

Evelyn
Lake

Long Meadow

Creek

Sunrise
Lakes

Nelson
Lake

RANGE

Sunrise

JOHN MUIR

Vogelsang

Vogelsang
Lake

N

Emeric
Lake

Vogelsang
Peak

0   Kilometers   2

0   Miles   2

Eichorn Pinnacle, Cathedral Peak

The aptly named Cathedral Peak is an eye-catching peak from almost any angle. The lower northern summit gives way to a gradual slope that ascends a mile or so to the abrupt tower of the true summit. Its shape really does suggest a European cathedral: Imagine climbing the side of the cathedral of Notre Dame in Paris and scaling the high point from the roof.

From the trailhead, follow the John Muir Trail south toward Cathedral Lakes. At a point about 2.5 miles in, just past a small pass, a use trail leads to the peak. Low angle and easy at first, the trail quickly steepens and moves up over gravel and blocks. Pick the easiest route through Class 3 slabs and talus, generally bearing left of center, to a point between Eichorn Pinnacle (the west summit, a freestanding tower) and the true summit.

An exposed series of ledges leads to the south side of the summit block. A short, blocky crack (Class 4 climbing) leads to the tiny summit. The difficult moves are short, with good solid stances every body length or so.

The first ascent of Cathedral Peak was completed by John Muir, who climbed it alone in 1869. At the time, it was considered the most difficult in the Sierra.

20. CLOUDS REST

Highlights: A one-of-a-kind peak and summit: a cross between a Tuolumne dome and a high-country mountain. This hike bridges the abyss between Tuolumne Meadows and Yosemite Valley, with this summit as its centerpiece. This is a classic mountain traverse, with the bonus of a view down onto the summit of Half Dome from a thousand feet above.

Clouds Rest

Distance: Mileages (all trail) for the four options are:
  Tuolumne Meadows to Yosemite Valley, one way, 24 miles.
  Tenaya Lake to Yosemite Valley, one way, 15 miles.
  From Tenaya Lake, round trip, 11miles.
  From Yosemite Valley, round trip, 20 miles.
Difficulty: Class 2+; strenuous.
Trailhead Elevations:
  Tuolumne Meadows: 8,700 feet
  Tenaya Lake: 8,152 feet
  Yosemite Valley: 3,900 feet
Summit Elevation: 9,926 feet
Elevation Gain:
  From Tuolumne Meadows: 1,226 feet
  From Tenaya Lake: 1,774 feet
  From Yosemite Valley: 6,026 feet
Best Months: June through September.
Maps: USGS Tenaya Lake; DeLorme *Northern California Atlas and Gazetteer*, page 111; National Geographic, Yosemite National Park.
Latitude: 37°44'45"N
Longitude: 119°31'59"W

Permits: None needed for day use; wilderness permit required for overnight stay. Entrance fee charged to enter Yosemite National Park.

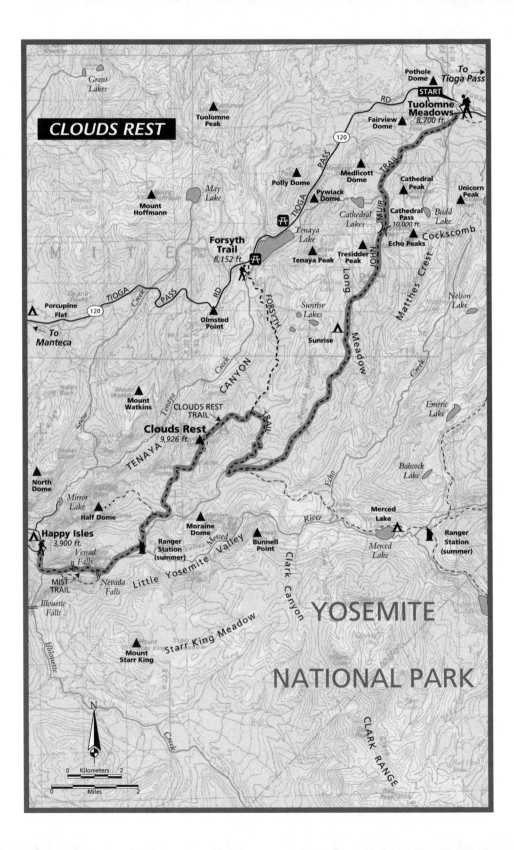

CLOUDS REST

To Tioga Pass →

Pothole Dome

START
Tuolomne Meadows
8,700 ft.

RD

Fairview Dome

Grant Lakes

Tuolomne Peak

Cathedral Peak

120

Polly Dome

Medlicott Dome

Unicorn Peak

TIOGA PASS

Pywiack Dome

Mount Hoffmann

May Lake

Cathedral Lakes

Cathedral Pass
10,000 ft.

Budd Lake

JOHN MUIR TRAIL

Echo Peaks

Cockscomb

Tenaya Lake

Tenaya Peak

Tresidder Peak

Matthes Crest

Nelson Lake

Forsyth Trail
8,152 ft.

Sunrise Lakes

TIOGA

Creek

PASS

RD

Olmsted Point

FORSYTH

CANYON

Sunrise

Long Meadow

Porcupine Flat

120

← To Manteca

Creek

Emeric Lake

Mount Watkins

CLOUDS REST TRAIL

FORSYTH TRAIL

Babcock Lake

TENAYA

Tenaya

Clouds Rest
9,926 ft.

North Dome

Snow

Echo

Merced Lake

Ranger Station (summer)

Mirror Lake

Half Dome

Moraine Dome

Merced Valley

Bunnell Point

River

Merced Lake

Happy Isles
3,900 ft.

Vernal Falls

Ranger Station (summer)

Little Yosemite Valley

Clark Canyon

MIST TRAIL

Nevada Falls

YOSEMITE

Illouette Falls

Illouette

Starr King Meadow

Mount Starr King

NATIONAL PARK

N

CLARK RANGE

Creek

0   Kilometers   2

0   Miles   2

Trailheads:

> Tuolumne Meadows—Cathedral Peak trailhead, 1 mile west of Tuolumne Meadows store.
>
> Tenaya Lake—at the campground at the west end of the lake.
>
> Yosemite Valley—at Happy Isles in the eastern end of the valley.

Clouds Rest is an overlooked classic. Although a thousand feet higher than Half Dome, it nonetheless hides in the background and is often overlooked by hikers and mountaineers. There are several ways to approach the climb of Clouds Rest, and four are described here.

The most aesthetic adventure takes a one-way, 24-mile route from Tuolumne Meadows to Clouds Rest and down to Yosemite Valley. A shorter one-way option starts at Tenaya Lake and ends in Yosemite Valley. Both of these routes require a car shuttle, or use of the bus from Yosemite Valley to the start of the hike.

You also have the options of a round-trip route to Clouds Rest from Yosemite Valley or a round-trip hike from Tenaya Lake.

For the ambitious hike from Tuolumne Meadows to the valley, start at the Cathedral Peak trailhead. Follow the John Muir Trail for 3 miles as it climbs to Cathedral Pass (10,000 feet), with Cathedral Peak displayed on your left. Next comes the aptly named 3.6-mile-long Long Meadow, from Cathedral Pass to Sunrise High Sierra Camp. You can refill your drinking water at nearby Sunrise Lakes, as long as you run it through a water filter or treat it chemically. The long, jagged ridge on your left is Matthes Crest, with Tresidder Peak on your right.

After almost a mile past Sunrise Camp, a trail junction is reached. Go right for Clouds Rest, on the Forsyth Trail. Follow this trail for 2.5 miles as it climbs to almost 10,000 feet before hitting another junction, where it joins the Clouds Rest Trail. Turn left here. After another 1.5 miles, you'll reach the rocky summit of Clouds Rest, at 9,926 feet. (An optional pack animal trail skirts the actual summit for the vertigo-challenged.) Take time to eat lunch and soak up the views, including the unusual perspective of the summit of Half Dome a thousand feet below. The vistas across upper Yosemite Valley of Quarter Dome, Basket Dome, and Mount Watkins are superb.

From here, follow the trail down 3.7 miles to its junction with the Half Dome Trail. Take the Half Dome Trail, which becomes the John Muir Trail, traveling through Little Yosemite Valley to the junction with the Mist Trail just above the top of Nevada Falls. Follow the Mist Trail for 2.5 miles, down past Vernal Falls to the Happy Isles trailhead at the eastern end of Yosemite Valley. From here, you can take a well-deserved bus ride to Curry Village. But if the buses have ended operations for the day, you can walk for another mile to Curry Village.

For the one-way hike from Tenaya Lake, take the Forsyth Trail, getting on it from the campground at the west end of the lake. Follow the trail for 4 miles to its junction with the Clouds Rest Trail. From here to Clouds Rest and down to the valley, the route is the same as the one already described, from Tuolumne Meadows.

Both of these one-way routes can serve as superlative trail runs. Trail runners who would like to make the route closer to the full marathon length of 26.2

miles can start from the Tuolumne Meadows store. The total distance to Happy Isles will still be a little short—but after crossing three points at or near an elevation of 10,000 feet, you won't feel cheated.

Hikers who prefer a round-trip hike, starting and ending at the same point, can begin at either Tenaya Lake or Yosemite Valley. The round trip from Tenaya Lake is 11 miles, with an elevation gain of 1,774 feet.

The round trip from Yosemite Valley is by far the steepest variation, with an elevation gain of more than 6,000 feet. From the Happy Isles trailhead, follow the Mist Trail past Vernal and Nevada Falls to its junction with the John Muir Trail just above Nevada Falls. Take this trail and then the Half Dome Trail to its junction with the Clouds Rest Trail, and from there it's 3.75 miles to the summit of Clouds Rest. Return the same way. (For a more detailed description of the route from Happy Isles to the Clouds Rest junction, see Half Dome, climb #21.)

21. HALF DOME

Highlights: A demanding hike; a unique ascent protected by metal cables; spectacular views far down into Yosemite Valley. Come on, it's Half Dome! A very popular route for trail runners, the standing round-trip record is about three hours and fifteen minutes—but most parties will be happy to do it in eight hours.
Distance: 16 miles round trip (all trail, except for the top section with the cables).
Difficulty: Class 3; moderate.
Trailhead Elevation: 3,900 feet
Summit Elevation: 8,836 feet
Elevation Gain: 4,936 feet
Best Months: June through September.
Maps: USGS Half Dome; DeLorme *Northern California Atlas and Gazetteer*, page 111; National Geographic, Yosemite National Park.
Latitude: 37°44'45"N
Longitude: 119°31'59"W
Permits: None needed for day use; wilderness permit required for overnight stay. Entrance fee charged to enter Yosemite National Park.
Trailhead: Yosemite Valley, at Happy Isles in the eastern end of the valley.

Half Dome is the second-highest point on the Yosemite Valley rim, exceeded only by Clouds Rest. Considering the terrain and the vertical gain—and the protective cables bolted into the final section to the top—this trip is as adventure-filled as anything in this book. Half Dome is a feature unique enough to be used as the logo for Yosemite National Park, a place with more unusual features than you can shake a giant sequoia stick at.

Steep and paved, the first mile of the trail from Happy Isles climbs to the base of Vernal Falls. There are bathrooms and drinking fountains at the bridge before the base of the falls.

Half Dome

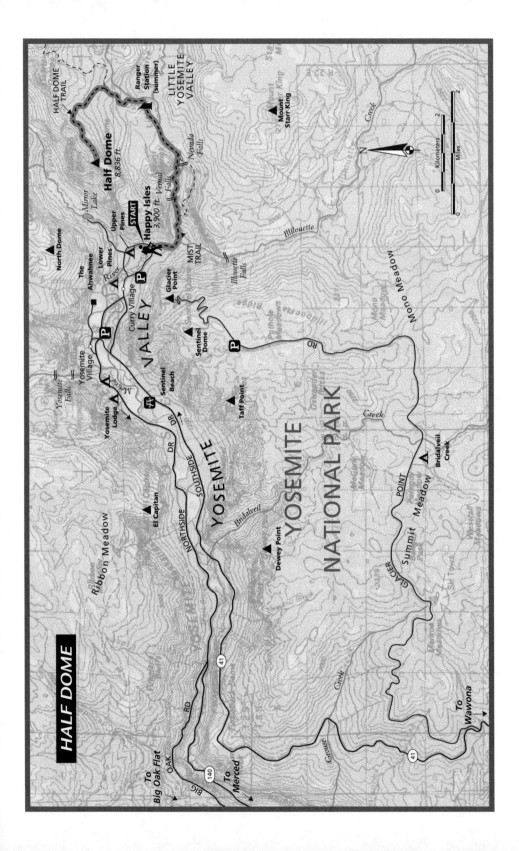

The trail continues to the top of Vernal Falls via the Mist Trail, ascending hewn granite steps immediately adjacent to the falls. In the spring, or almost anytime in a heavy rain year, you will get soaked on this aptly named trail. Above Vernal Falls, the trail ascends to the top of Nevada Falls, where there is a solar bathroom but no drinking water.

For the next 4 miles the trail levels off somewhat and passes through Little Yosemite Valley, where there is a backpackers' campground and another environment-friendly toilet facility. Soon you'll reach a trail sign that says Half Dome 2.2 miles. Now the climb begins in earnest.

Steep hiking leads to a challenging, exposed scramble up a bare and rocky shoulder to the base of the cables, which ascend the smooth eastern side of Half Dome. Without the cables, the ascent here would be a technical, Class 5 friction climb up steep granite. The two cables serve as handrails, and wooden two-by-fours are in place on the granite between each pair of cable posts—providing access to a summit that would otherwise be solely the realm of rock climbers.

The austere summit is a rocky plain covering several acres—a fragile, heavily visited environment. Staying on top overnight is not permitted; it's said that six of the seven trees that once grew here were used up as firewood. Take time to look over the edge at the forbidding northwest face; you may even see climbers on the route, one of the most famous in Yosemite.

High Sierra

The Sierra Nevada range is almost 400 miles long and more than 50 miles wide. Most of the highest peaks are reached from the east side of the range, south of Yosemite, via Highway 395 through Owens Valley.

The range uplifts abruptly on the east, making for steep approaches with great elevation gain. These are big mountains: Most climbs involve a round trip of 8 to 10 miles and more, with several thousand feet of elevation gain and loss, sometimes with mountaineering or routefinding challenges. The weather can change dramatically over the course of a day. It can be over a hundred degrees down in the valley at Bishop while the summit of Split Mountain, nearly 10,000 feet higher, is below freezing. Always come to the High Sierra prepared for cold weather.

22. MAMMOTH MOUNTAIN

Highlights: A broad, monolithic peak looming above the town of Mammoth Lakes. Of the eye-arresting summits in the area as seen from Highway 395, Mammoth is the big, wide one. Offering a relatively easy hike, it is a fine introduction to the high country and a good orientation to the area.

Distance: 8 miles round trip (all trail).

Difficulty: Class 2; easy.

Trailhead Elevation: 9,000 feet

Summit Elevation: 11,053 feet

Elevation Gain: 2,053

Best Months: June through September, depending on snow conditions.

Maps: USGS Mammoth Mountain; DeLorme *Northern California Atlas and Gazetteer*, page 112; Tom Harrison, Mammoth High Country.

Latitude: 37°37'51"N

Longitude: 119°01'54"W

Permits: None needed for day use; wilderness permit required for overnight stay.

Trailhead: From the town of Mammoth Lakes, follow the signs to the Mammoth Mountain Ski Area. The marked trailhead is near the west end of the parking lot.

Take the trail designed for hikers only—but even then, watch out for mountain bikes. The trail starts in the shade of large Jeffrey pines and soon winds around the north and west sides of the peak in open country. The trail reaches the top from the west.

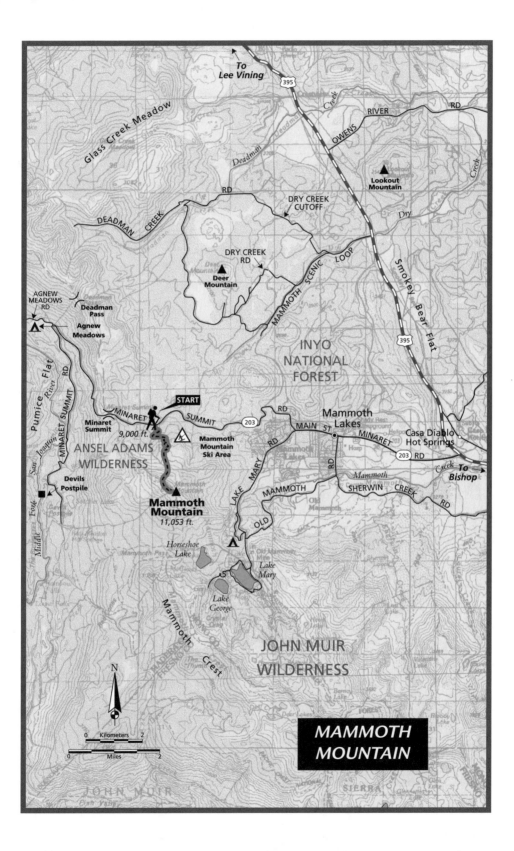

To
Lee Vining

395

Creek

OWENS RIVER RD

Deadman

Glass Creek Meadow

Deadman

RD

DRY CREEK
CUTOFF

Lookout
Mountain

Dry

Creek

DEADMAN CREEK

DRY CREEK
RD

Deer
Mountain

Mammoth Scenic Loop

Smokey Bear Flat

395

INYO
NATIONAL
FOREST

AGNEW
MEADOWS
RD

Deadman
Pass

Agnew
Meadows

Pumice Flat

Minaret Summit RD

San Joaquin River

MINARET   SUMMIT

START

Minaret
Summit
9,000 ft.

203

RD

Mammoth
Mountain Ski Area

MAIN ST.

Mammoth
Lakes

MINARET

Casa Diablo
Hot Springs

203 RD

ANSEL ADAMS
WILDERNESS

Devils
Postpile

Mammoth
Mountain
11,053 ft.

LAKE MARY RD

RD

MAMMOTH

OLD

Mammoth
SHERWIN CREEK RD

Creek

To
Bishop

Middle Fork

Horseshoe
Lake

Old Mammoth

Lake
Mary

Lake
George

Mammoth Crest

MADERA FREEWAY

JOHN MUIR
WILDERNESS

N

Kilometers
0   2

Miles
0   2

JOHN MUIR   SIERRA

**MAMMOTH
MOUNTAIN**

You'll be rewarded with views of the Minarets, the Ritter Range, and Devil's Postpile. This is a good acclimatization hike for the beginning of a trip (or season) of peak-bagging. Hike back down, or ride the gondola to descend.

23. MOUNT RITTER (NORTH FACE)

Highlights: The highest point of the Ritter Range, with views of the central Sierra, Mono Lake, and into Nevada. This is a prominent notch-backed mountain, a compelling sight from Highway 395. Ritter is a challenging peak, requiring some technical climbing experience.

Distance: 9 miles round trip (all trail, except for short sections across snowfields).

Difficulty: Class 3; strenuous; bring an ice ax, and also consider crampons.

Trailhead Elevation: 8,400 feet

Summit Elevation: 13,157 feet

Elevation Gain: 4,757 feet

Best Months: June through September.

Maps: USGS Mount Ritter; DeLorme *Northern California Atlas and Gazetteer*, pages 111 and 112; Tom Harrison, Mammoth High Country.

Latitude: 37°41'22"N

Longitude: 119°11'53"W

Permits: None needed for day use; wilderness permit required for overnight stay.

Trailhead: Agnew Meadows. From the town of Mammoth Lakes, drive to the main ski area at Mammoth Mountain. Between 7:30 A.M. and 5:30 P.M., private

Mount Ritter (left) and Banner Peak (right) from Lake Ediza

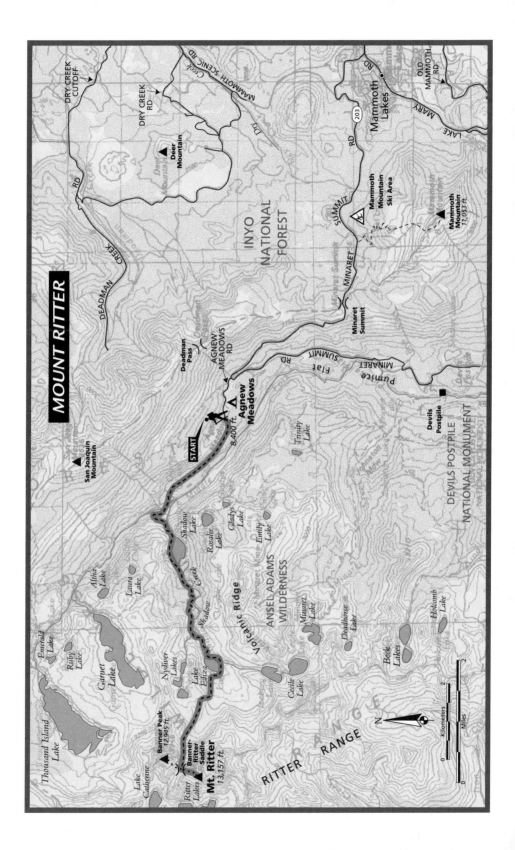

MOUNT RITTER

Thousand Island Lake

Emerald Lake

Ruby Lake

Garnet Lake

Lake Catherine

Ritter Lakes

▲ Banner Peak 12,945 ft.

Banner-Ritter Saddle

▲ Mt. Ritter 13,157 ft.

Nydiver Lakes

Lake Ediza

Shadow Creek

Cecile Lake

Minaret Lake

Deadhorse Lake

RITTER   RANGE

Beck Lakes

Holcomb Lake

Alpha Lake

Laura Lake

Shadow Lake

Rosalie Lake

Gladys Lake

Emily Lake

Volcanic Ridge

ANSEL ADAMS WILDERNESS

Trinity Lake

San Joaquin Mountain ▲

START

8,400 ft.

Agnew Meadows

Deadman Pass

AGNEW MEADOWS RD

DEADMAN   CREEK

DRY CREEK CUTOFF

DRY CREEK RD

Deer Mountain ▲

RD

MAMMOTH SCENIC RD

INYO

NATIONAL

FOREST

Minaret Summit

Flat MINARET SUMMIT RD

Pumice

SUMMIT RD

MINARET

203

Mammoth Lakes

LAKE MARY RD

OLD MAMMOTH RD

Mammoth Mountain Ski Area

▲ Mammoth Mountain 11,053 ft.

Devils Postpile ■

DEVILS POSTPILE NATIONAL MONUMENT

N

Kilometers   0   2

Miles   0   2

vehicles are prohibited from the road between the ski area and Agnew Meadows; take the shuttle bus to the trailhead at Agnew Meadows.

Take full precautions against bears in this area. Bear-proof food canisters are mandatory for backpackers; they can be rented locally.

Mount Ritter is a big mountain and a serious undertaking. Two steep snowfields must be crossed, and they can be treacherous when icy. From the Agnew Meadows trailhead, the trail goes north for 3.5 miles of rolling and often downhill terrain to Shadow Lake. From here the trail turns west and climbs abruptly, then levels off to Lake Ediza, 3.2 miles from Shadow Lake. Designated campsites are available in this area.

The summit of Mount Ritter is 2.3 miles from Lake Ediza. To ascend the north face of Ritter, climb from the lake to the Banner–Ritter Saddle. The route is straightforward and steep. A low-angle snowfield leads to Class 3 rock that ascends to the saddle. From the saddle, climb a steeper and potentially hazardous snowfield. Three climbable chutes lead up from here, with the one farthest west (right) the easiest and most solid. From the top of the chute, follow a wide ramp up to an *arête* (ridge). Follow this, or traverse farther left to another chute, to the summit.

Most climbing parties hike in to Lake Ediza, camp, and climb Mount Ritter and Banner Peak on the next day or the next two days.

24. BANNER PEAK

Highlights: A logical companion peak to Mount Ritter. Banner Peak is somewhat shorter and technically easier. Fine views from the summit.
Distance: 9 miles round trip (about 7.5 miles on trail and 1.5 miles of off-trail scrambling, with a short snowfield section).
Difficulty: Class 3; strenuous; ice ax may be needed.
Trailhead Elevation: 8,400 feet
Summit Elevation: 12,945 feet
Elevation Gain: 4,545 feet
Best Months: June through September.
Maps: USGS Mount Ritter; DeLorme *Northern California Atlas and Gazetteer*, pages 111 and 112; Tom Harrison, Mammoth High Country.
Latitude: 37°41'48"N
Longitude: 119°11'39"W
Permits: None needed for day use; wilderness permit required for overnight stay.
Trailhead: Agnew Meadows. From the town of Mammoth Lakes, drive to the main ski area at Mammoth Mountain. Between 7:30 A.M. and 5:30 P.M., private vehicles are prohibited from the road between the ski area and Agnew Meadows; take the shuttle bus to the trailhead at Agnew Meadows.

Take full precautions against bears in this area. Bear-proof food canisters are mandatory for backpackers; they can be rented locally.

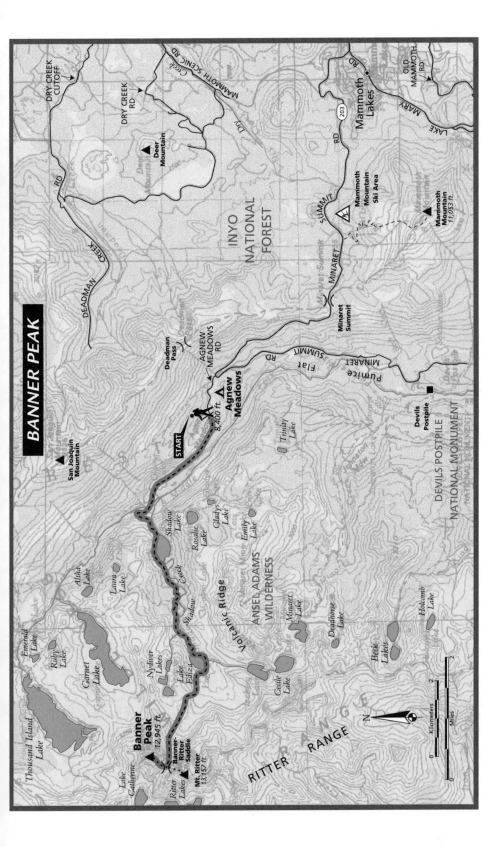

BANNER PEAK

Though not as technically difficult as Mount Ritter, Banner Peak still presents a long climb. The route from Agnew Meadows to Lake Ediza is the same: From the trailhead, it heads north for 3.5 miles to Shadow Lake, then turns uphill and proceeds another 3.2 miles to Lake Ediza.

From this lake, climb to the Banner–Ritter Saddle. The route crosses a low-angle snowfield where an ice ax may be needed. The snowfield leads to Class 3 rock that ascends to the saddle. From the saddle, it's a straightforward Class 2 scramble to the summit of Banner.

Most climbing parties hike in to Lake Ediza, camp, and climb Mount Ritter and Banner Peak on the next day or the next two days.

25. MOUNT MORRISON

Highlights: A spectacular-looking peak from Highway 395, with a 3,000-foot-high buttress on display.

Distance: 8 miles round trip (all trail).

Difficulty: Class 3; moderate; potentially dangerous due to loose rock.

Trailhead Elevation: 7,621 feet

Summit Elevation: 12,268 feet

Elevation Gain: 4,647 feet

Best Months: June through September.

Maps: USGS Convict Lake; DeLorme *Northern California Atlas and Gazetteer*, page 112; Tom Harrison, Mammoth High Country.

Latitude: 37°33'42"N

Longitude: 118°51'32"W

Mount Morrison

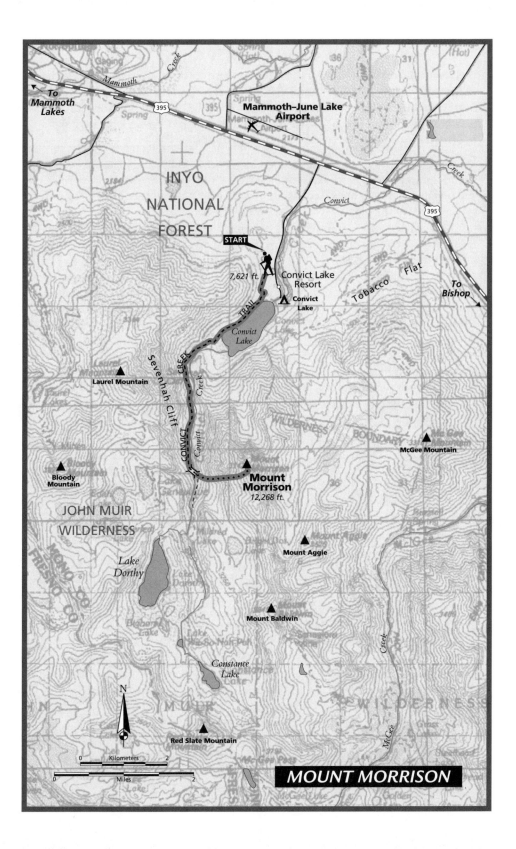

To Mammoth Lakes

Mammoth–June Lake Airport

INYO NATIONAL FOREST

START

7,621 ft.

Convict Lake Resort

Convict Lake

Tobacco Flat

To Bishop

TRAIL

Convict Lake

Sevenhah Cliff

CREEK

Creek

Laurel Mountain

WILDERNESS BOUNDARY

McGee Mountain

CONVICT

Convict

Bloody Mountain

Mount Morrison
12,268 ft.

JOHN MUIR WILDERNESS

Lake Dorthy

Mount Aggie

Mount Baldwin

Constance Lake

WILDERNESS

Creek

McGee

N

Red Slate Mountain

MUIR

0 Kilometers 2

0 Miles 2

MOUNT MORRISON

Permits: None needed for day use; wilderness permit required for overnight stay.
Trailhead: On Highway 395, travel 4.5 miles south from the Mammoth Lakes
turnoff (or 10.5 miles north from Tom's Place) to the Convict Lake turnoff.
From the highway, drive three-quarters of a mile toward Convict Lake to the
trailhead, which is marked with a sign on the right.

Mount Morrison is an immense peak visible for many miles and easily accessible
from Highway 395. The peak, especially the east-facing buttress, appears solid
and impressive. Looks are deceiving, however. The mountain is perhaps the loos-
est slag heap in the Sierra, with lots of unstable rock.

The mountain offers many climbing routes, one of which bears the nickname
Eiger of the Sierra, due to the danger involved in an ascent. The safest and easiest route is from the west.

From the trailhead, follow the Convict Creek Trail southwest up a small rise
and then down to Convict Lake. The trail then follows around the lake and into
a canyon behind Mount Morrison. The trail rises up the canyon to a bridge about
3 miles from the lake. Cross the bridge and turn left (east) and slog up loose
talus in a long, wide slot.

There are several ways to go here. Most parties will want to keep to the rocky
ledges on the right side of the gully, as it appears to be the most stable. Follow
this to the summit. This is the south summit, the actual high point of the mountain. But don't go up when it's wet, and therefore slippery. To descend, carefully
reverse your steps.

26. MOUNT STARR (EAST SLOPE)

Highlights: Quickest summit in the Rock Creek area—a good ascent if you
have only a short time there or want a brief introduction to the local layout.
Incredible views from the summit.
Distance: 4.4 miles round trip (about half on trail, half off-trail scrambling).
Difficulty: Class 2; moderate.
Trailhead Elevation: 9,695 feet
Summit Elevation: 12,835 feet
Elevation Gain: 3,140 feet
Best Months: June through September.
Maps: USGS Mount Abbot; DeLorme *Northern California Atlas and Gazetteer*,
page 123; Tom Harrison, Mono Divide High Country.
Latitude: 37°25'37"N
Longitude: 118°45'54"W
Permits: None needed for day use; wilderness permit required for overnight
stay.
Trailhead: Mosquito Flat. Heading south on Highway 395, south of Mammoth
Lakes, turn west onto Rock Creek Road at a sign marked Tom's Place, just
before the highway drops toward Bishop. The trailhead is at Mosquito Flat at

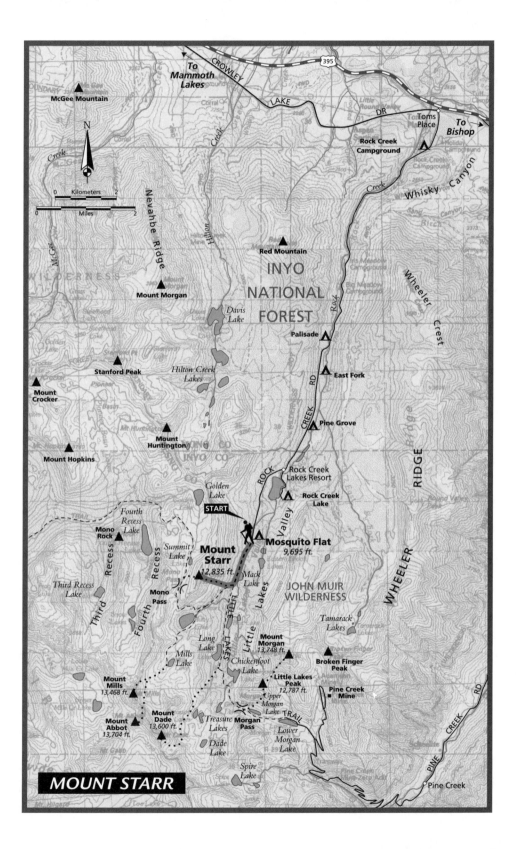

MOUNT STARR

East slope, Mount Starr

the very end of the road, 11 miles from Highway 395, just past the Rock Creek Resort.

Mount Starr is the quickest-to-reach summit in the region. If you have limited time, this is the peak to climb. Atop the summit, you can savor all the surrounding peaks.

From the trailhead, hike up Little Lakes Valley for about half a mile to Mack Lake. At the junction by the lake, go right toward Mono Pass. But after only about a quarter-mile up the Mono Pass Trail, find a use trail to the right that heads up the east slope of Mount Starr. Follow this loose trail to the ridge and take the ridge to the summit.

You can also ascend the west side of Starr, directly from Mono Pass. This route is of similar difficulty, but with not as much loose rock. It's about 3 miles from Mack Lake to Mono Pass.

27. MOUNT MORGAN
(VIA LITTLE LAKES PEAK)

Highlights: Easily accessible from a high trailhead, with great views of the Rock Creek–area peaks, especially Bear Creek Spire. Mount Morgan is the large, sweeping peak on the left when looking from the trailhead.

Distance: 9.6 miles round trip (about 8 miles on trail, about 1.5 miles of off-trail scrambling).

Difficulty: Class 3; moderate.

Trailhead Elevation: 9,695 feet

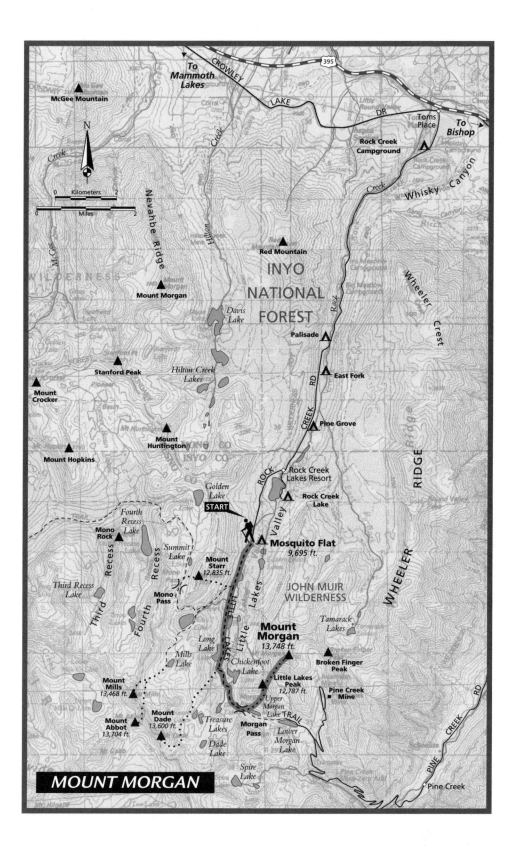

MOUNT MORGAN

Mount Morgan

Summit Elevation: 13,748 feet
Elevation Gain: 4,053 feet
Best Months: June through September.
Maps: USGS Mount Morgan; DeLorme *Northern California Atlas and Gazetteer*, page 123; Tom Harrison, Mono Divide High Country.
Latitude: 37°24'20"N
Longitude: 118°43'59"W
Permits: None needed for day use; wilderness permit required for overnight stay.
Trailhead: Mosquito Flat. Heading south on Highway 395, south of Mammoth Lakes, turn west onto Rock Creek Road at a sign marked Tom's Place, just before the highway drops toward Bishop. The trailhead is at Mosquito Flat at the very end of the road, 11 miles from Highway 395, just past the Rock Creek Resort.

Mosquito Flat provides a fine trailhead at almost 10,000 feet that affords easier access to high peaks than anywhere in the Sierra save Tuolumne Meadows. Mount Morgan is the easiest climb among the major peaks in the Rock Creek Basin.

From the trailhead (take bug spray), hike in pines up the Little Lakes Valley, following signs for Morgan Pass. From Morgan Pass climb across the scree and up Little Lakes Peak, keeping to the right of Class 5 slabs. From the summit of Little Lakes Peak (12,782 feet), follow the ridge (Class 3 blocks) to the summit of Mount Morgan.

28. MOUNT MILLS (EAST COULOIR)

Highlights: A dramatic peak offering superlative views. Mount Mills, Mount Abbot, and Mount Dade, when viewed from the Rock Creek Basin, present a wall of peaks irresistible to the mountaineer.

Distance: 8.2 miles round trip (about half on trail, half off trail).

Difficulty: Class 3; moderate/strenuous; may require ice ax in early season.

Trailhead Elevation: 9,695 feet

Summit Elevation: 13,468 feet

Elevation Gain: 3,773 feet

Best Months: June through September.

Maps: USGS Mount Abbot; DeLorme *Northern California Atlas and Gazetteer*, page 123; Tom Harrison, Mono Divide High Country.

Latitude: 37°23'36"N

Longitude: 118°47'19"W

Permits: None needed for day use; wilderness permit required for overnight stay.

Trailhead: Mosquito Flat. Heading south on Highway 395, south of Mammoth Lakes, turn west onto Rock Creek Road at a sign marked Tom's Place, just before the highway drops toward Bishop. The trailhead is at Mosquito Flat at the very end of the road, 11 miles from Highway 395, just past the Rock Creek Resort.

Mount Mills is the northernmost peak of the dramatic Mills–Abbot–Dade trifecta, rising above Little Lakes Valley. From Mosquito Flat take the Mono Pass Trail about 1.6 miles to Ruby Lake. A use trail on the east side leads about 1.3 miles to Mills Lake and the Mills–Abbot glacier beyond.

Skirting the glacier along its eastern margin, climb a large couloir (gully), the East Couloir, seemingly blocked by a large chockstone. Getting past the chockstone is the crux and may require an ice ax. Climb the chute above to the summit plateau and follow south to the summit.

To descend, reverse your route, returning down the east couloir. As an alternative descent route, you can traverse the ridge south toward Mount Abbot and descend Class 3 ledges to the Mills–Abbot Couloir. Cross the Mills–Abbot glacier and rejoin the extension of the use trail used on the ascent.

29. MOUNT ABBOT (NORTH COULOIR)

Highlights: A spectacular peak in a spectacular setting, part of the Mills–Abbot–Dade trio.

Distance: 8.4 miles round trip (about half on trail, half off trail).

Difficulty: Class 3; strenuous; requires ice ax.

Trailhead Elevation: 9,695 feet

Summit Elevation: 13,704 feet

Elevation Gain: 4,009 feet

Best Months: June through September.

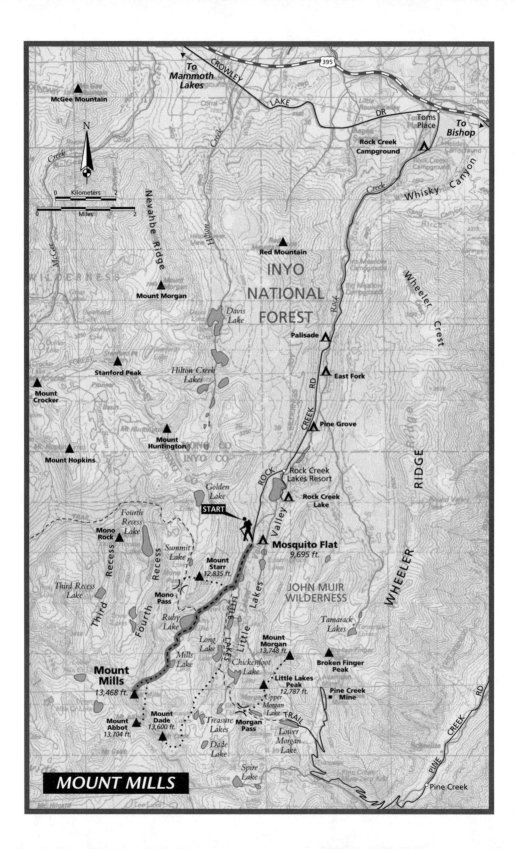

MOUNT MILLS

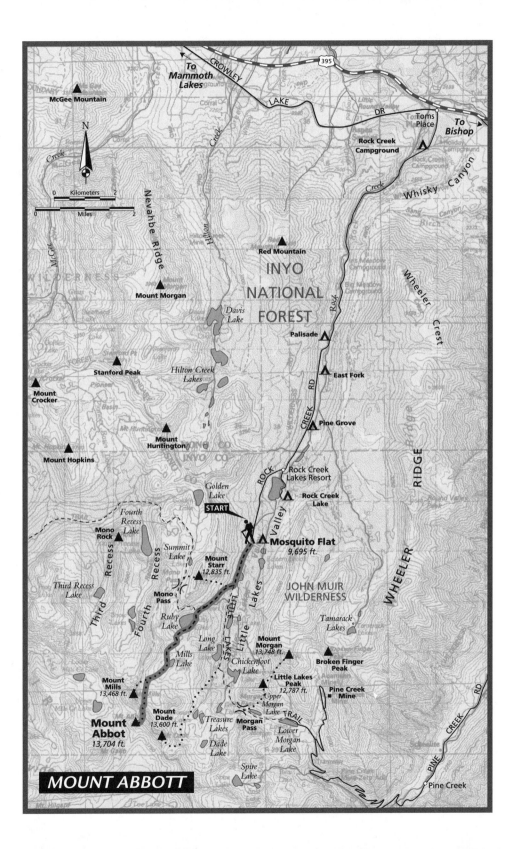

Maps: USGS Mount Abbot; DeLorme *Northern California Atlas and Gazetteer*, page 123; Tom Harrison, Mono Divide High Country.
Latitude: 37°23′10″N
Longitude: 118°47′00″W
Permits: None needed for day use; wilderness permit required for overnight stay.
Trailhead: Mosquito Flat. Heading south on Highway 395, south of Mammoth Lakes, turn west onto Rock Creek Road at a sign marked Tom's Place, just before the highway drops toward Bishop. The trailhead is at Mosquito Flat at the very end of the road, 11 miles from Highway 395, just past the Rock Creek Resort.

Mount Abbot is the middle peak of the dramatic group formed by Mounts Mills, Abbot, and Dade, which rises above Little Lakes Basin.

From Mosquito Flat take the Mono Pass trail to Ruby Lake, about 1.6 miles. A use trail on the east side leads 1.3 miles to Mills Lake and the Mills–Abbot glacier beyond. From here climb the North Couloir, a prominent snow-filled gully north of a rocky buttress. About halfway up the couloir (before the snow gets steep), exit right on Class 3 rock. Follow this to the northwest ridge, and follow the ridge to the summit of Abbot.

To descend, traverse the ridge north toward Mount Mills and descend Class 3 ledges to the Mills–Abbot Couloir. Cross the Mills–Abbot glacier and rejoin the extension of the use trail used on the ascent.

30. MOUNT DADE (THE HOURGLASS)

Highlights: Moderate snow climbing and mixed scrambling, making for an enjoyable and varied day. Dade is a member of the striking trio of Mount Mills, Mount Abbot, and Mount Dade.
Distance: 8.8 miles round trip (about half on trail, half off trail).
Difficulty: Class 2–3 strenuous; requires ice ax in early season.
Trailhead Elevation: 9,695 feet
Summit Elevation: 13,600 feet
Elevation Gain: 3,905 feet
Best Months: June through September.
Maps: USGS Mount Abbot; DeLorme *Northern California Atlas and Gazetteer*, page 123; Tom Harrison, Mono Divide High Country.
Latitude: 37°22′54″N
Longitude: 118°46′42″W
Permits: None needed for day use; wilderness permit required for overnight stay.
Trailhead: Mosquito Flat. Heading south on Highway 395, south of Mammoth Lakes, turn west onto Rock Creek Road at a sign marked Tom's Place, just before the highway drops toward Bishop. The trailhead is at Mosquito Flat at the very end of the road, 11 miles from Highway 395, just past the Rock Creek Resort.

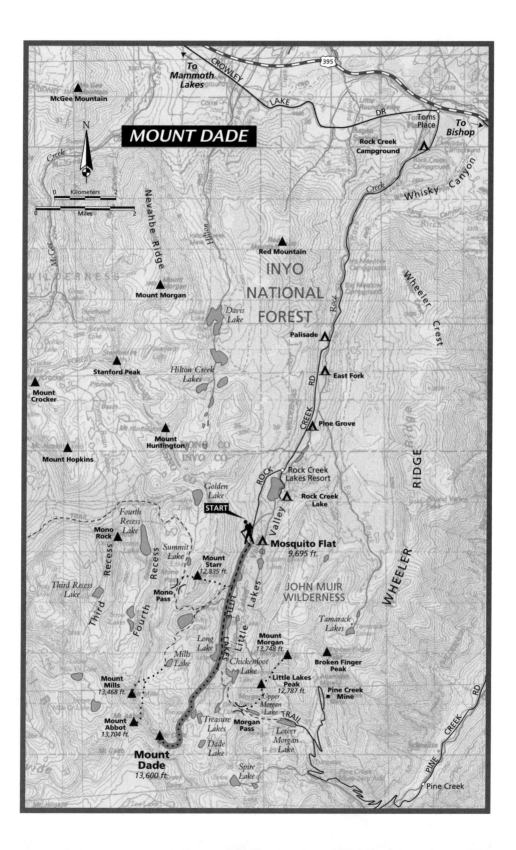

Mount Dade is the southernmost of the adjoining peaks of Mills, Abbot, and Dade. Its distinctive feature is the couloir (gully) known as the Hourglass, named for its upper and lower flare and middle taper.

From Mosquito Flat, take the Little Lakes Trail for about 3 miles, past Long Lake to a point between Long Lake and Chickenfoot Lake. From here a use trail leads to Treasure Lakes in a little under 1.5 miles.

From Treasure Lakes, scramble up into the snow- or scree-filled Hourglass couloir on the south side of Mount Dade. The couloir is flanked on both sides by steeper, rocky buttresses. Follow the Hourglass to the top of the cirque (a semi-encircling rock wall), then follow the ridge to the summit.

31. MOUNT TOM (FROM HORTON LAKE)

Highlights: A huge peak (the biggest) as seen from the town of Bishop. Mount Tom commands views of the Sierra Nevada, the Owens Valley, and the White Mountains.

Distance: 14 miles round trip (10 miles on trail, 4 miles off trail).

Difficulty: Class 2; strenuous.

Trailhead Elevation: 8,000 feet

Summit Elevation: 13,652 feet

Elevation Gain: 5,652 feet

Best Months: June through September, but often longer depending on snow conditions.

Maps: USGS Mount Tom; DeLorme *Northern California Atlas and Gazetteer*, page 123.

Mount Tom (right) and Basin Mountain (left)

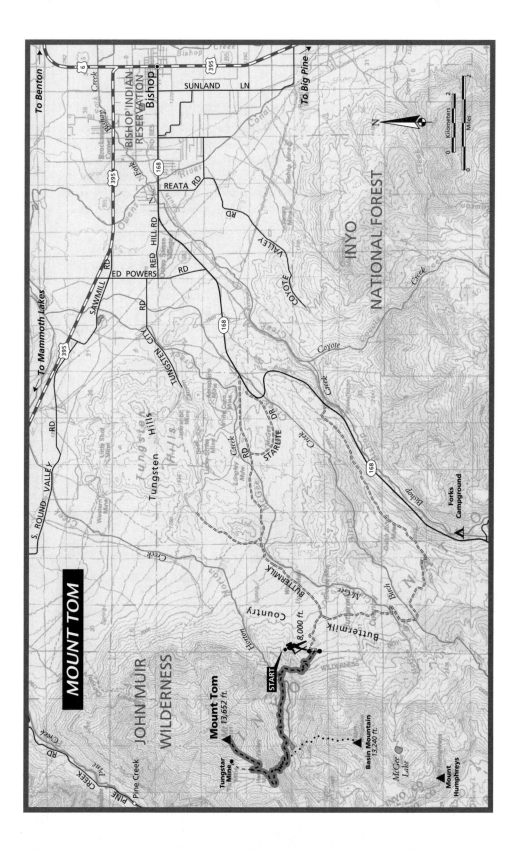

Latitude: 37°20'19"N
Longitude: 118°39'27"W
Permits: None needed for day use; wilderness permit required for overnight stay.
Trailhead: From Bishop, drive west on Highway 168 about 7 miles to Buttermilk Road. The pavement ends after about one hundred yards. Stay on the main, most heavily used road, and ignore various minor side tracks that obviously get little traffic. Take the right fork at mile 1.8 on Buttermilk Road, then take the left fork at mile 3.5. After 6 miles there is a fork to the right with a sign that says Horton. Take this right-hand fork and drive a short way to a locked gate.

Mount Tom is big. It's large when seen from Highway 395, down in the Owens Valley—and it seems even bigger when you're cresting the false summits near the top. The route, however, is straightforward. From the locked gate at the trailhead, follow the steep trail (an old, dirt, mining road) for 4 miles through trees and meadows and past old buildings to Horton Lake.

From Horton Lake, another old road leads up a steep hillside to the Tungstar Mine, an abandoned tungsten mine. Leave the road where it crosses the southwest ridge and follow this up across talus to the summit. Keep slightly below the ridgeline on the way.

32. BASIN MOUNTAIN (NORTH SLOPE)

Highlights: A companion to Mount Tom, offering panoramic views. From Bishop and Highway 395, Basin Mountain can be seen as the blocky, multifaceted peak south of the monolithic Mount Tom.
Distance: 13.5 miles round trip (about 8 miles on dirt road, the remainder on trail with some off-trail).
Difficulty: Class 2; moderate.
Trailhead Elevation: 8,000 feet
Summit Elevation: 13,240 feet
Elevation Gain: 5,240 feet
Best Months: June through September, but often much later depending on snow conditions.
Maps: USGS Mount Tom; DeLorme *Northern California Atlas and Gazetteer*, page 123.
Latitude: 37°17'50"N
Longitude: 118°39'28"W
Permits: None needed for day use; wilderness permit required for overnight stay.
Trailhead: From Bishop, drive west on Highway 168 about 7 miles to Buttermilk Road. The pavement ends after about one hundred yards. Stay on the main, most heavily used road, and ignore various minor side tracks that obviously get little traffic. Take the right fork at mile 1.8 on Buttermilk Road, then take the left fork at mile 3.5. After 6 miles there is a fork to the right with a sign that says Horton. Take this right-hand fork and drive a short way to a locked gate.

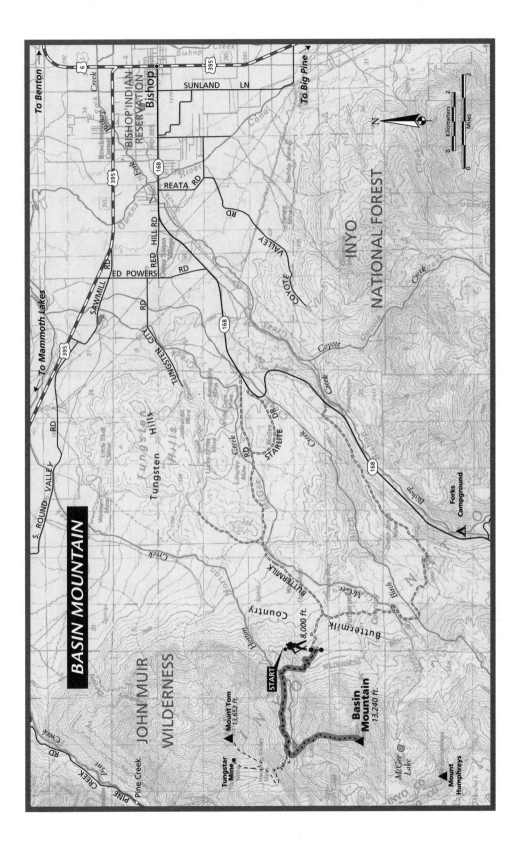

BASIN MOUNTAIN

JOHN MUIR WILDERNESS

INYO NATIONAL FOREST

BISHOP INDIAN RESERVATION

Bishop

SUNLAND LN

To Benton

To Big Pine

To Mammoth Lakes

REATA RD

RED HILL RD

RED POWERS RD

SAWMILL RD

TUNGSTEN CITY RD

Tungsten Hills

STARLITE DR

COYOTE VALLEY

S. ROUND VALLEY

PINE CREEK RD

Pine Creek

▲ Mount Tom
13,652 ft.

Tungstar Mine

BUTTERMILK Country

8,000 ft.

START

Horton

Creek

McGee

Birch

Buttermilk

WILDERNESS

▲ Basin Mountain
13,240 ft.

McGee Lake

▲ Mount Humphreys

Forks Campground

Bishop

N

Kilometers

Miles

Basin Mountain

From the locked gate at the trailhead, follow the steep trail (actually an old, dirt, mining road) for 4 miles as it winds its way in and out of trees, meadows, and past old mining-claim buildings to Horton Lake. From Horton Lake turn south on a good use trail and climb the north face directly. The east summit is the highest point.

33. MOUNT EMERSON (FROM PIUTE PASS)

Highlights: A large, intriguing mountain, the east end of which is covered with red spires (the Piute Crags). The route makes for a good trail run, with the bonus of great views along the way. The peak was named by John Muir for his friend Ralph Waldo Emerson.

Distance: 13 miles round trip (10 miles on trail, 3 miles off trail).

Difficulty: Class 3; strenuous.

Trailhead Elevation: 9,400 feet

Summit Elevation: 13,204 feet

Elevation Gain: 3,804 feet

Best Months: June through September.

Maps: USGS Mount Darwin; DeLorme *Northern California Atlas and Gazetteer*, page 123; Tom Harrison, Mono Divide High Country.

Latitude: 37°14'32"N

Longitude: 118°39'09"W

Permits: None needed for day use; wilderness permit required for overnight stay.

Trailhead: North Lake. From Bishop, take Highway 168 west, following the signs for Lake Sabrina. About 18 miles from Bishop, and about 1 mile before

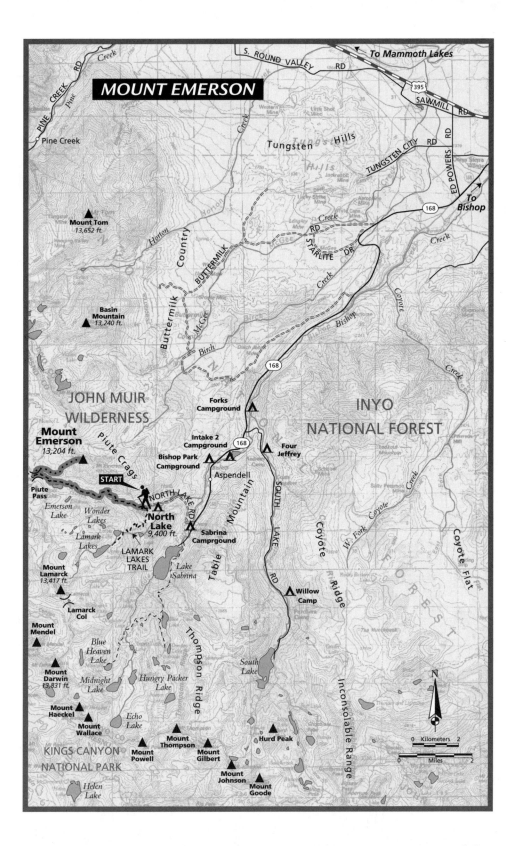

MOUNT EMERSON

To Mammoth Lakes

S. ROUND VALLEY RD

SAWMILL RD

395

To Bishop

168

ED POWERS RD

TUNGSTEN CITY RD

Tungsten Hills

Hills

STARLITE DR

Pine Creek

PINE CREEK RD

Pine Creek

Horton *Creek*

Creek

Western Mine

Little Shot Mine

Coyote Creek

Bishop *Creek*

168

Mount Tom
13,652 ft.

BUTTERMILK RD

Buttermilk Country

McGee Creek

Birch Creek

Basin Mountain
13,240 ft.

JOHN MUIR WILDERNESS

Mount Emerson
13,204 ft.

Piute Crags

START

Piute Pass

Emerson Lake

Wonder Lakes

Lamark Lakes

NORTH LAKE RD

North Lake
9,400 ft.

Forks Campground

Intake 2 Campground

168

Bishop Park Campground

Aspendell

Four Jeffrey

INYO NATIONAL FOREST

Sabrina Campground

Lake Sabrina

Table Mountain

SOUTH LAKE RD

Coyote Ridge

W. Fork Coyote Creek

Coyote Flat

LAMARK LAKES TRAIL

Mount Lamarck
13,417 ft.

Lamarck Col

Mount Mendel

Blue Heaven Lake

Willow Camp

Mount Darwin
13,831 ft.

Midnight Lake

Hungry Packer Lake

Thompson Ridge

South Lake

Mount Haeckel

Mount Wallace

Echo Lake

Mount Powell

Mount Thompson

Mount Gilbert

Hurd Peak

Inconsolable Range

F O R E S T

N

KINGS CANYON NATIONAL PARK

Mount Johnson

Mount Goode

Helen Lake

0   Kilometers   2

0   Miles   2

Lake Sabrina, a road with a sign for North Lake branches off right and climbs abruptly. There is a sign and toilet at the North Lake trailhead.

From North Lake, take the trail to Piute Pass, which goes up a wide valley in a mixed conifer forest. The trail climbs a steep, rocky step before coming to the lake known as Loch Leven. Before the lake you are confronted on your right with the Piute Crags, a bizarre assortment of craggy spires that would, by themselves, make the hike memorable. A sought-after goal for rock climbers, the crags offer Class 5 climbing. The trail levels off again before starting the grind up to Piute Lake. Wildlife is abundant in this valley, especially deer, squirrels, and bears.

Another grade takes you up to Piute Pass, 5 miles from the North Lake trailhead. From the pass, hike northeast to a plateau to the west of Mount Emerson, where you'll find many small lakes. From here climb to the northwest summit and traverse the ridge to the true high point, the south summit.

34. MOUNT LAMARCK

Highlights: Beautiful route in spectacular terrain. The ascent provides for a long day of hiking, with a substantial elevation gain. Mount Lamarck serves as a good introduction to the Evolution region of the Sierra.

Distance: 12 miles round trip (11 miles on trail, 1 mile off trail).

Difficulty: Class 2; moderate.

Trailhead Elevation: 9,400 feet

Summit Elevation: 13,417 feet

Elevation Gain: 4,017 feet

Best Months: June through September.

Maps: USGS Mount Darwin; DeLorme *Northern California Atlas and Gazetteer*, page 123; Tom Harrison, Mono Divide High Country.

Latitude: 37°11'42"N

Longitude: 118°40'13"W

Permits: None needed for day use; wilderness permit required for overnight stay.

Trailhead: North Lake. From Bishop, take Highway 168 west, following the signs for Lake Sabrina. About 18 miles from Bishop, and about 1 mile before Lake Sabrina, a road with a sign for North Lake branches off right and climbs abruptly. There is a sign and toilet at the North Lake trailhead.

It's no coincidence that both Mount Lamarck and Mount Darwin are in the Evolution region of the Sierra. Mount Lamarck is named for Jean-Baptiste Lamarck, the French botanist and zoologist whose theory of evolution was one of the inspirations for Darwin's own theory. Science is a stern taskmaster, however. Though Lamarck is lauded for distinguishing between animals with and without backbones and for other contributions to science, he is most remembered for his theory of the inheritance of acquired characteristics, which was turned on its head by the acceptance of Darwin's own theory of evolution through natural selection. But at least Lamarck got a peak named after him.

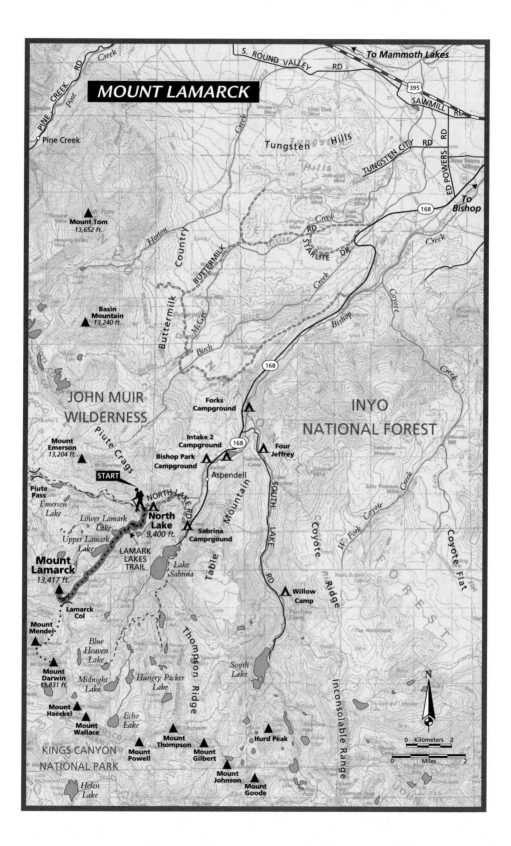

From the North Lake trailhead, take the Lamarck Lakes Trail. Leave the trail from a point between Upper and Lower Lamarck Lakes, about 2.3 miles from the trailhead, near where the trail crosses a stream. Follow a use trail across a meadow.

The trail steepens until it reaches a wide, sandy valley dotted with boulders. A tiny lake sits just below Lamarck Col (pass). Ascend to the col by climbing past snowfields to the first notch to the right of a small crag. Then ascend Class 2 terrain along the ridge to the summit.

35. MOUNT DARWIN (WEST RIDGE)

Highlights: The thematic and topographic keystone of the Evolution region. Mount Darwin is a large peak that dominates the area, just as Darwin's theory of evolution stands high in science. The way this classic route crosses the margin of a glacier and circles around the ridge and up to the summit makes for an elegant climbing experience. It's a must-do climb in the Evolution region.

Distance: 20 miles round trip (11 miles on trail, 9 miles off trail).

Difficulty: Class 3; strenuous.

Trailhead Elevation: 9,128 feet

Summit Elevation: 13,831 feet

Elevation Gain: 4,703 feet

Best Months: June through October.

Maps: USGS Mount Darwin; DeLorme *Northern California Atlas and Gazetteer*, page 123; Tom Harrison, Mono Divide High Country.

Latitude: 37°10'01"N

Longitude: 118°41'04"W

Permits: None needed for day use; wilderness permit required for overnight stay.

Trailhead: North Lake. From Bishop, take Highway 168 west, following the signs for Lake Sabrina. About 18 miles from Bishop, and about 1 mile before Lake Sabrina, a road with a sign for North Lake branches off right and climbs abruptly. There is a sign and toilet at the North Lake trailhead.

This is a long climb, and many parties bivouac around Lamarck Col or in Darwin Canyon. From the trailhead, take the Lamarck Lakes Trail. Leave the trail from a point between Upper and Lower Lamarck Lakes, about 2.3 miles from the trailhead, near where the trail crosses a stream. Follow a use trail across a meadow.

The trail steepens until it reaches a wide, sandy valley dotted with boulders. A tiny lake sits just below Lamarck Col (pass). Ascend to the col by climbing past snowfields to the first notch to the right of a small crag. To this point the route is the same as for Mount Lamarck.

Now proceed across the col and down the other side into Darwin Canyon. From here ascend the west ridge—the rock ridge to the right (west) of the glacier. Follow the ridge to the summit plateau. If you keep to the right of the glacier, it's possible to avoid glacier travel and the need to carry ice ax and crampons.

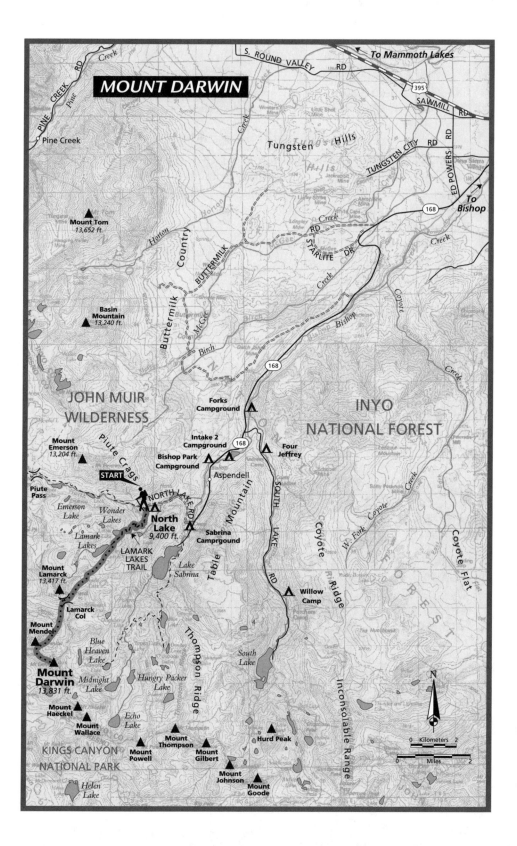

MOUNT DARWIN

To Mammoth Lakes

S. ROUND VALLEY RD

395

SAWMILL RD

Pine Creek

PINE CREEK RD

Creek

Pine

Creek

Tungsten Hills

Hills

TUNGSTEN CITY RD

ED POWERS RD

To Bishop

168

▲ **Mount Tom**
13,652 ft.

Horton

Buttermilk Country

BUTTERMILK

Creek

McGee RD

STARLITE DR

168

Creek

Coyote

▲ **Basin Mountain**
13,240 ft.

McGee

Buttermilk

Birch

Bishop

Creek

Birch

Creek

N

JOHN MUIR WILDERNESS

Piute Crags

168

Forks Campground ▲

INYO NATIONAL FOREST

Creek

▲ **Mount Emerson**
13,204 ft.

Intake 2 Campground ▲

168

Four Jeffrey ▲

START

Bishop Park Campground ▲

NORTH LAKE RD

Aspendell

Piute Pass

Emerson Lake

Wonder Lakes

North Lake
9,400 ft.

Table Mountain

SOUTH LAKE RD

Coyote Ridge

W. Fork Coyote

Coyote Flat

Lamark Lakes

Sabrina Camprgound ▲

▲ **Mount Lamarck**
13,417 ft.

LAMARK LAKES TRAIL

Lake Sabrina

Willow Camp ▲

Lamarck Col

Thompson Ridge

Blue Heaven Lake

South Lake

F O R E S T

▲ **Mount Mendel**

Midnight Lake

Hungry Packer Lake

▲ **Mount Darwin**
13,831 ft.

▲ **Mount Haeckel**

Echo Lake

▲ **Mount Wallace**

▲ **Mount Thompson**

Hurd Peak ▲

Inconsolable Range

N

KINGS CANYON NATIONAL PARK

▲ **Mount Powell**

▲ **Mount Gilbert**

0   Kilometers   2

0   Miles   2

Helen Lake

▲ **Mount Johnson**

▲ **Mount Goode**

The very summit of the peak is a small detached pinnacle on the southeast side of the summit plateau. A Class 3 crack on the west side of the pinnacle leads to the summit. (Many parties call it good when they reach the summit plateau.)

36. HURD PEAK

Highlights: A hidden gem, with a short approach. Hurd Peak makes for a beautiful climb, and is perfect for those with limited time.

Distance: About 7 miles round trip (5 miles on trail, 2 miles of off-trail scrambling).

Difficulty: Class 3; moderate.

Trailhead Elevation: 9,768 feet

Summit Elevation: 12,237 feet

Elevation Gain: 2,469 feet

Best Months: June through September.

Maps: USGS Mount Thompson; DeLorme *Northern California Atlas and Gazetteer*, page 123.

Latitude: 37°08′29″N

Longitude: 118°33′55″W

Permits: None needed for day use; wilderness permit required for overnight stay.

Trailhead: South Lake. From Bishop, take Highway 168 west for 15 miles, following the signs for Lake Sabrina. About 3 miles before Lake Sabrina, a road with a sign for South Lake branches left near the Forks Campground. Take this road for about 6 miles, to its end.

Hurd Peak

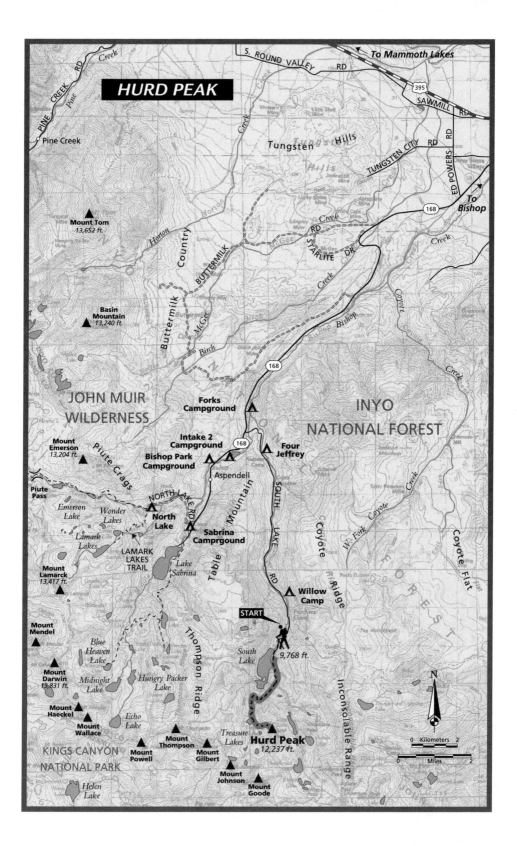

HURD PEAK

To Mammoth Lakes

Pine Creek

PINE CREEK RD

Pine Creek

Mount Tom
13,652 ft.

Tungsten Hills

S. ROUND VALLEY RD

SAWMILL RD

395

Tungsten City RD

TUNGSTEN CITY RD

ED POWERS RD

168

To Bishop

STARLITE DR

Horton

Horton Country

BUTTERMILK

Basin Mountain
13,240 ft.

Buttermilk

McGee

Birch

Bishop

Coyote

168

Creek

JOHN MUIR WILDERNESS

INYO NATIONAL FOREST

Piute Crags

Mount Emerson
13,204 ft.

Forks Campground

Intake 2 Campground

168

Four Jeffrey

Bishop Park Campground

Aspendell

Piute Pass

Emerson Lake

Wonder Lakes

NORTH LAKE RD

North Lake

Table Mountain

Sabrina Camprgound

SOUTH LAKE RD

Coyote

W. Fork Coyote

Coyote Flat

Lamark Lakes

LAMARK LAKES TRAIL

Lake Sabrina

Mount Lamarck
13,417 ft.

Mount Mendel

Blue Heaven Lake

Thompson Ridge

Willow Camp

START

9,768 ft.

Inconsolable Range

Mount Darwin
13,831 ft.

Midnight Lake

Hungry Packer Lake

South Lake

Mount Haeckel

Echo Lake

Mount Wallace

Mount Thompson

Treasure Lakes

Hurd Peak
12,237 ft.

KINGS CANYON NATIONAL PARK

Mount Powell

Mount Gilbert

Helen Lake

Mount Johnson

Mount Goode

N

Kilometers 2

Miles 2

From the trailhead, Hurd Peak is in full view ahead. The route, however, is hidden on the opposite side of the peak. Take the trail past South Lake as it winds around south and west to Treasure Lakes, about 2.5 miles from the trailhead.

The climb starts from here. From the lake, ascend the west face of Hurd Peak, threading your way between blocks and spires. Several Class 3 options are apparent for the final section to the summit.

37. MOUNT GAYLEY (SOUTHWEST RIDGE)

Highlights: One of the few peaks in the Palisades area that offers a nontechnical route to the summit. As a relatively low-key ascent in an area of high and steep-sided peaks, Gayley is much sought-after by hikers and climbers.
Distance: About 15 miles round trip (14 miles on trail, 1 mile off trail).
Difficulty: Class 3; strenuous; ice ax required for a few moves to Glacier Notch.
Trailhead Elevation: 8,000 feet
Summit Elevation: 13,510 feet
Elevation Gain: 5,510 feet
Best Months: June through September.
Maps: USGS Split Mountain; DeLorme *Northern California Atlas and Gazetteer*, page 123; Tom Harrison, Kings Canyon High Country.
Latitude: 37°06'11"N
Longitude: 118°29'58"W
Permits: None needed for day use; wilderness permit required for overnight stay.
Trailhead: Glacier Lodge trailhead. From the town of Big Pine, drive west on Crocker Street, which becomes Glacier Lodge Road. Follow the road for 13.5

Photo: U.S. Geological Survey/Matthes, F. E. 1289

Mount Gayley from the north

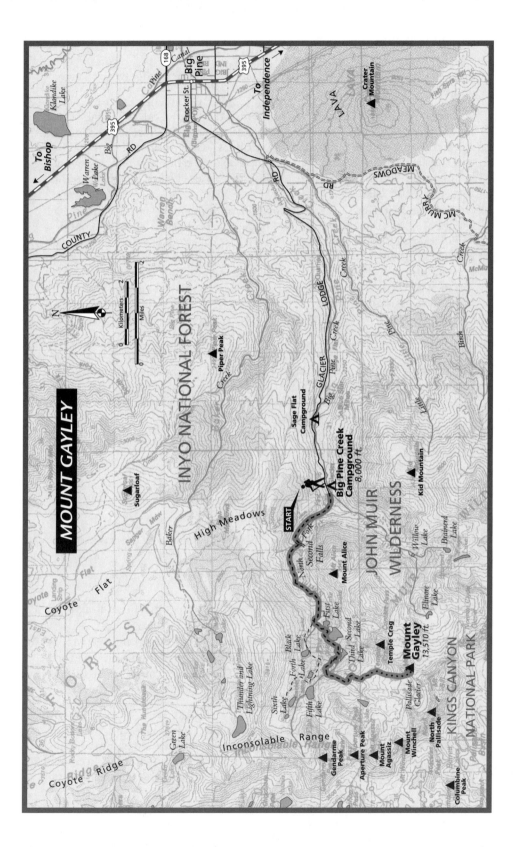

MOUNT GAYLEY

To Bishop

To Independence

Klondike Lake

Warren Lake

Big Pine Canal

Big Pine

Crocker St.

168

395

INYO NATIONAL FOREST

COUNTY

RD

Warren Bench

Sugarloaf

Piper Peak

Baker

Spring Mdw

High Meadows

Coyote Flat

FOREST

Coyote Ridge

Green Lake

Thunder and Lightning Lake

The Hermit

Inconsolable Range

Sixth Lake

Fifth Lake

Forth Lake

Black Lake

Second Falls

North Fork

First Lake

Second Lake

Third Lake

Sage Flat Campground

Big Pine Creek Campground
8,000 ft.

START

Mount Alice

GLACIER

LODGE

RD

Big Pine Creek

Pine Creek

Little Pine Creek

McMur

Birch Creek

MCMURRY MEADOWS

LAVA

Crater Mountain

High Sierra Trail

Kid Mountain

Willow Lake

Brainerd Lake

JOHN MUIR WILDERNESS

Elinore Lake

Temple Crag

Mount Gayley
13,510 ft.

Palisade Glacier

North Palisade

Mount Winchell

Mount Agassiz

Aperture Peak

Gendarme Peak

Columbine Peak

KINGS CANYON NATIONAL PARK

N

Kilometers
0   1   2

Miles
0   1   2

miles to the trailhead at the end of the road, near Glacier Lodge, where a sign indicates parking for hikers.

From the trailhead, follow the trail west along the North Fork of Big Pine Creek toward Palisade Glacier. A junction with a dead-end trail is reached at about 1.8 miles; stay on the main trail. The trail continues past the waterfall known as Second Falls and up onto a flat plateau (where a stone cabin south of the trail was built by actor Lon Chaney in 1925). Hike past a series of lakes: First Lake, Second Lake, and Third Lake.

One mile past Third Lake is the junction with the Sam Mack Meadows trail, about 6.3 miles from the trailhead. Follow this trail south across the meadow and up the ridge below the edge of the Palisade Glacier. Hike over rocks and slabs past the northwest rib of Mount Gayley, making toward Glacier Notch, a pass between Mount Gayley and Mount Sill. Some scrambling and possible snow (if you need an ax, it will be here) lead to the pass. Ascend the peak via the ridge from Glacier Notch.

38. SPLIT MOUNTAIN

Highlights: The second-easiest ascent of a 14,000-foot mountain in the Sierra (Mount Muir is the easiest). The large cleft separating the north and south summits makes this peak easily identifiable from down in Owens Valley. Split Mountain is an increasingly popular alternative to the crowded Mount Whitney, especially for hikers with four-wheel-drive vehicles.

Distance: 18 miles round trip (all trail).

Difficulty: Class 3; strenuous.

Trailhead Elevation: 6,400 feet

Summit Elevation: 14,058 feet

Elevation Gain: 7,658 feet

Best Months: June through September.

Maps: USGS Split Mountain; DeLorme *Northern California Atlas and Gazetteer*, page 123; Tom Harrison, Kings Canyon High Country.

Latitude: 37°01′16″N

Longitude: 118°25′20″W

Permits: None needed for day use; wilderness permit required for overnight stay.

Trailhead: From Big Pine on Highway 395, drive west on Crocker Street. About 2.5 miles from Big Pine, immediately after a bridge, turn left on a dirt road and follow signs to the Red Mountain trailhead. This is a very rough road that has gotten worse in recent years, requiring a high-clearance vehicle with four-wheel drive.

Split Mountain, although technically easy, is a long, steep climb and makes for a lengthy day. From the trailhead, hike 6 miles to Red Lake on the unmaintained trail. The trail is in a state of decline, so pay attention to routefinding. From Red Lake, hike northwest past its inlet for 2 miles up inclines and talus to the Split

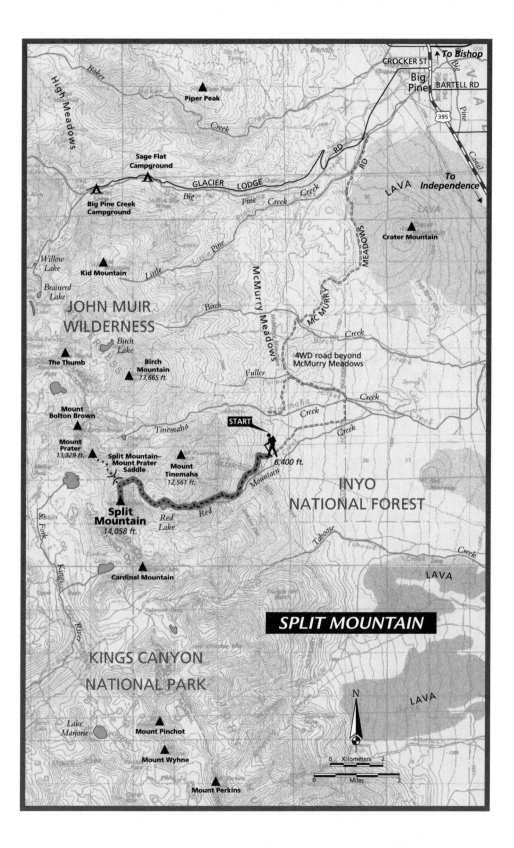

SPLIT MOUNTAIN

Mountain–Mount Prater saddle. From the saddle, hike up the long north ridge to the summit of Split Mountain.

You can make this strenuous hike less of a survival test by camping overnight at Red Lake. That could also provide time to climb the companion to Split Mountain, Mount Prater, which is easily reached via the same saddle (see Mount Prater, climb #39).

39. MOUNT PRATER

Highlights: A companion peak to Split Mountain, or a fine climb in its own right.
Distance: 14 miles round trip (all trail).
Difficulty: Class 3; strenuous.
Trailhead Elevation: 6,400 feet
Summit Elevation: 13,329 feet
Elevation Gain: 6,929 feet
Best Months: June through September.
Maps: USGS Split Mountain; DeLorme *Northern California Atlas and Gazetteer*, page 123; Tom Harrison, Kings Canyon High Country.
Latitude: 37°02′15″N
Longitude: 118°26′08″W
Permits: None needed for day use; wilderness permit required for overnight stay.
Trailhead: From Big Pine on Highway 395, drive west on Crocker Street. About 2.5 miles from Big Pine, immediately after a bridge, turn left on the dirt road and follow signs to the Red Mountain trailhead. This is a very rough road that requires a high-clearance vehicle with four-wheel drive.

The long and strenuous route to the top of Mount Prater follows the trail to Split Mountain for most of the way. From the trailhead, hike 6 miles to Red Lake. This trail is not maintained and is in a state of decline, so pay attention to routefinding.

From Red Lake, hike 2 miles northwest to the Split Mountain–Mount Prater saddle. From the saddle, hike north along the ever-narrowing ridge to the summit of Mount Prater. The ridge is easier to negotiate than it first appears.

You have the option of camping overnight at Red Lake to spread the hike over two days. You can also climb to the top of Split Mountain, next to Mount Prater, from the same saddle (see Split Mountain, climb #38).

40. BIRCH MOUNTAIN (SOUTH SLOPE)

Highlights: A striking eastside peak, a neighbor to Mount Tinemaha (see climb #41). Birch Mountain provides a longer, higher ascent than Tinemaha—something for hikers wanting a little more.
Distance: About 13 miles round trip (10 miles on trail, 3 miles off trail).
Difficulty: Class 2; strenuous.
Trailhead Elevation: 6,400 feet

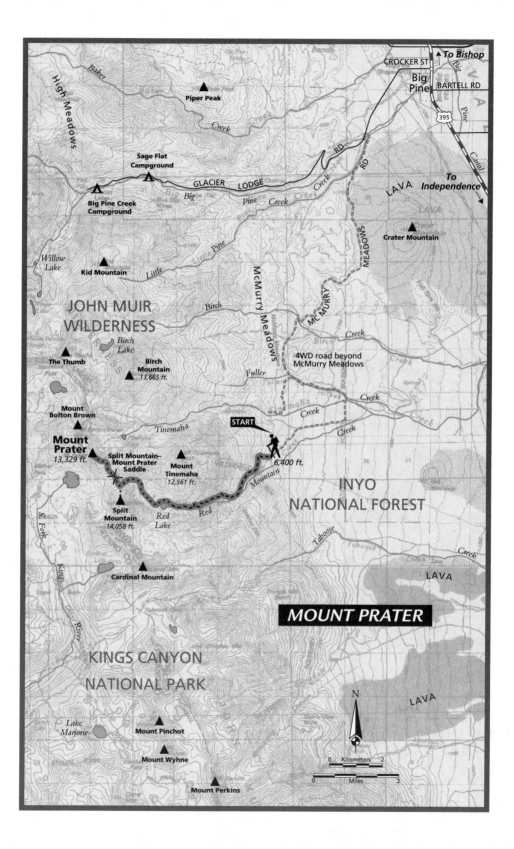

To Bishop

CROCKER ST

Big Pine

BARTELL RD

395

To Independence

Piper Peak

Sage Flat Campground

GLACIER LODGE

Big Pine Creek Campground

LAVA

LAVA

Crater Mountain

MEADOWS

Willow Lake

Kid Mountain

McMurry Meadows

McMURRY RD

4WD road beyond McMurry Meadows

JOHN MUIR WILDERNESS

Birch Lake

The Thumb

Birch Mountain
13,665 ft.

Fuller

Creek

Mount Bolton Brown

Mount Prater
13,329 ft.

Tinemaha

START

6,400 ft.

Split Mountain–
Mount Prater Saddle

Mount Tinemaha
12,561 ft.

Mountain

INYO NATIONAL FOREST

Split Mountain
14,058 ft.

Red Lake

Red

Taboose

Creek

LAVA

Cardinal Mountain

MOUNT PRATER

S. Fork

Kings

River

KINGS CANYON

NATIONAL PARK

LAVA

Lake Marjorie

Mount Pinchot

N

Mount Wyhne

0   Kilometers   2

Mount Perkins

0   Miles   2

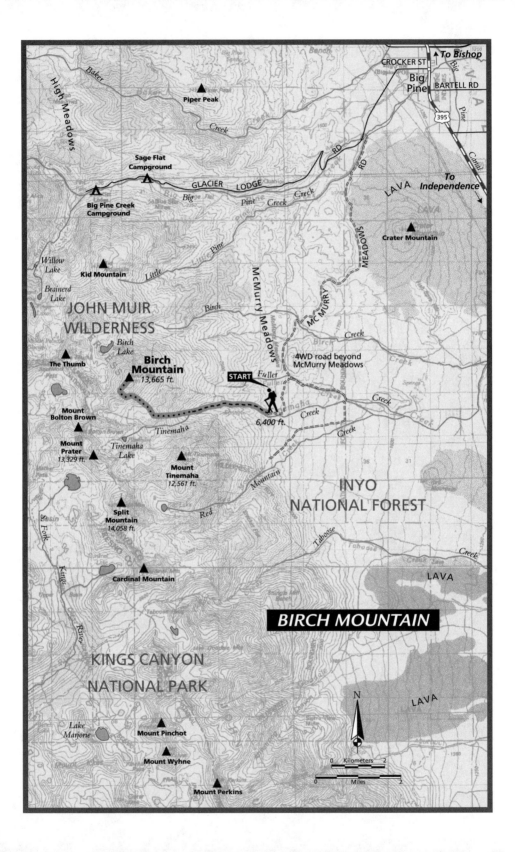

BIRCH MOUNTAIN

Summit Elevation: 13,665 feet
Elevation Gain: 7,265 feet
Best Months: June through September.
Maps: USGS Split Mountain; DeLorme *Northern California Atlas and Gazetteer*, page 123; Tom Harrison, Kings Canyon High Country.
Latitude: 37°03'50"N
Longitude: 118°25'05"W
Permits: None needed for day use; wilderness permit required for overnight stay.
Trailhead: McMurray Meadows. From Big Pine on Highway 395, head west on Crocker Street. After 2.5 miles, take a dirt road to the left, just after a bridge. Follow the signs toward the Red Mountain trailhead, but at a point 13 miles after the bridge, turn right (where the other route goes left) and drive a short way and park. The road gets steep and very sandy and continues a scant quarter-mile farther; walk this last quarter-mile to the trailhead.

From the trailhead, continue to hike west on the road as it rises some more, then drops down along Tinemaha Creek, becoming a use trail. Take this trail up as it follows the creek leading to Tinemaha Lake. Hike west in the valley between Birch Mountain and Mount Tinemaha. About 5 miles from the trailhead, shortly before reaching Tinemaha Lake, you'll come to the point that gives the easiest climbing up the south slope. Look for a trough between two series of rounded ridges. Follow this trough north through sage and scree and talus to the summit of Birch Mountain.

41. MOUNT TINEMAHA (EAST RIDGE)

Highlights: A complex, picturesque peak on the eastern crest overlooking Owens Valley. Its multipeaked summit can be seen for a long way and is often mistaken for Split Mountain (but it doesn't have that one major cleft that distinguishes Split Mountain).
Distance: About 5 miles round trip (3 miles on trail, 2 miles off trail).
Difficulty: Class 2; moderate.
Trailhead Elevation: 6,400 feet
Summit Elevation: 12,561 feet
Elevation Gain: 6,161 feet
Best Months: June through September.
Maps: USGS Split Mountain; DeLorme *Northern California Atlas and Gazetteer*, page 123; Tom Harrison, Kings Canyon High Country.
Latitude: 37°02'10"N
Longitude: 118°23'47"W
Permits: None needed for day use; wilderness permit required for overnight stay.
Trailhead: McMurray Meadows. From Big Pine on Highway 395, head west on Crocker Street. After 2.5 miles, take a dirt road to the left, just after a bridge.

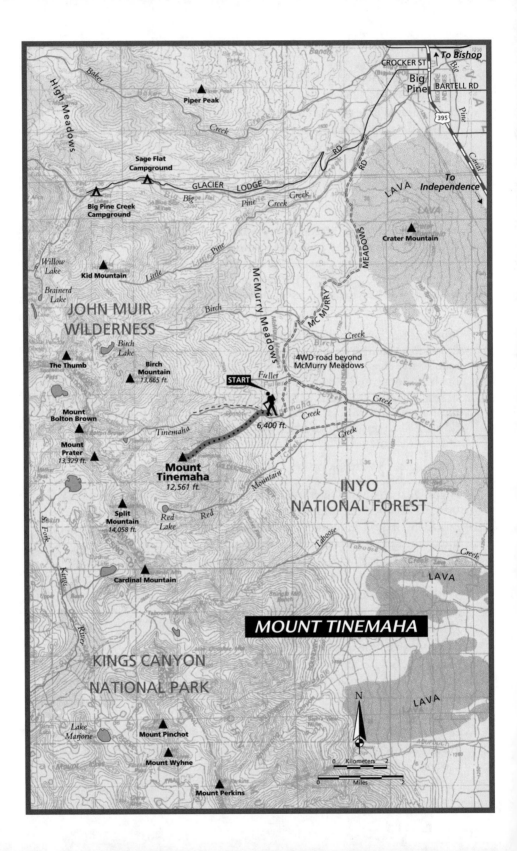

Mount Tinemaha

Follow the signs toward the Red Mountain trailhead, but at a point 13 miles after the bridge, turn right (where the other route goes left) and drive a short way and park. The road gets steep and very sandy and continues a scant quarter-mile farther; walk this last quarter-mile to the trailhead.

From the end of the dirt road at McMurray Meadows, it's a straightforward ascent up the east ridge of Mount Tinemaha. Follow the trail west for half a mile or so until it is practical to drop south and head directly west up the peak. Thread your way through blocks to the summit.

As an alternative route, you can ascend the south slope of Tinemaha from Red Lake. (See Split Mountain, climb #38, for the route to Red Lake.) It's also a straightforward ascent from the lake.

Mount Whitney Area

The Mount Whitney area is a land of contrasts, mostly topographic. The road to Whitney Portal climbs 4,000 feet in only 13 miles, leading from the desert at the town of Lone Pine into the High Sierra. Above Whitney Portal, cliffs soar thousands of feet high. Clean, bleached-white Sierra granite is the rule. Most of the peaks in the Whitney area are climbed from Whitney Portal, though several are accessed from roads out of the town of Independence, 16 miles north of Long Pine on Highway 395.

In this setting is Mount Whitney, highest point in the contiguous United States. All the peaks in the area are high, and much of the terrain is above tree line. The mountains here are distinctive: massive Lone Pine Peak; Mount Whitney, with its sheer east face; Mount Russell, with its long ridge; the spires of Mounts LeConte, Mallory, and Irvine. This is a peak-climber's paradise.

With paradise comes some consequences and restrictions. The Mount Whitney Trail is the most heavily used in the Sierra, with much traffic all season long. Where this many people go, the bears go as well. All of this has led to a firm permit system.

42. KEARSARGE PEAK

Highlights: Possibly the quickest-to-reach significant summit on the entire eastern side of the Sierra.
Distance: About 4 miles round trip (mostly off trail).
Difficulty: Class 2; easy/moderate.
Trailhead Elevation: 9,200 feet
Summit Elevation: 12,598 feet
Elevation Gain: 3,398 feet
Best Months: June through September.
Maps: USGS Kearsarge Peak; DeLorme *Southern California Atlas and Gazetteer*, page 26; Tom Harrison, Kings Canyon High Country.
Latitude: 36°47'21"N
Longitude: 118°20'47"W
Permits: None needed for day use; wilderness permit required for overnight stay.
Trailhead: Onion Valley Trailhead. From the town of Independence on Highway 395, drive west for 14 miles on Onion Creek Road and follow signs to the Onion Valley trailhead, where there's a parking area and campground.

Kearsarge Peak is quick work from the Onion Valley trailhead. But although the distance is short, don't forget that there is over 3,000 feet of elevation to be

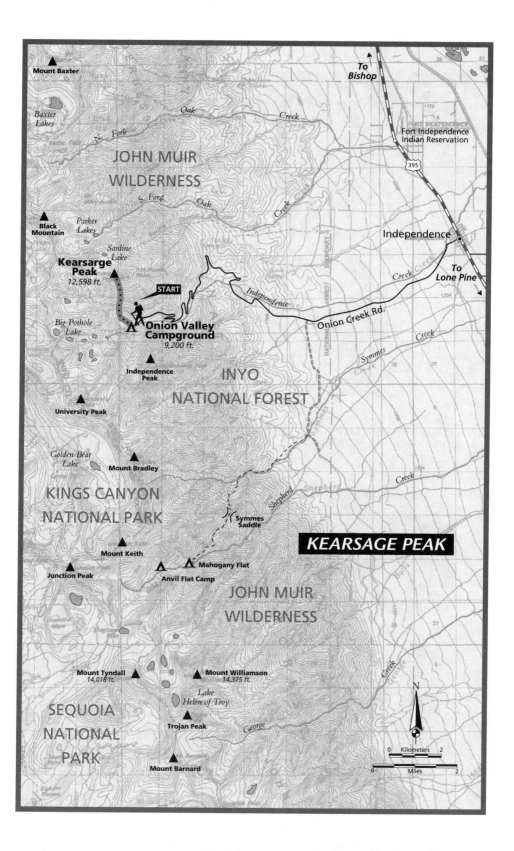

Mount Baxter

Baxter Lakes

JOHN MUIR WILDERNESS

N. Fork *Oak* *Creek*

S. Fork *Oak* *Creek*

To Bishop

Fort Independence Indian Reservation

395

Independence

To Lone Pine

Black Mountain

Parker Lakes

Sardine Lake

Kearsarge Peak
12,598 ft.

START

Onion Valley Campground
9,200 ft.

Big Pothole Lake

Independence *Creek*

Onion Creek Rd.

Independence Peak

INYO NATIONAL FOREST

University Peak

Symmes *Creek*

Golden Bear Lake

Mount Bradley

KINGS CANYON NATIONAL PARK

Shepherd *Creek*

Symmes Saddle

Mount Keith

KEARSAGE PEAK

Junction Peak

△ **Mahogany Flat**

△ **Anvil Flat Camp**

JOHN MUIR WILDERNESS

Mount Tyndall
14,018 ft.

Mount Williamson
14,375 ft.

Lake Helen of Troy

SEQUOIA NATIONAL PARK

Trojan Peak

George *Creek*

Mount Barnard

N

Kilometers
0   2

Miles
0   2

Kearsarge Peak

gained. From the trailhead, hike almost directly north and pick your route up the south side of this peak.

43. MOUNT WILLIAMSON (WEST FACE)

Highlights: The second-highest peak in California, after Whitney, and fifth-highest in the contiguous United States.

Distance: About 30 miles round trip (29 miles on trail, 1 mile off trail).

Difficulty: Class 3; very strenuous.

Trailhead Elevation: 5,600 feet

Summit Elevation: 14,375 feet

Elevation Gain: 8,775 feet

Best Months: May to mid-July.

Maps: USGS Mount Williamson; DeLorme *Southern California Atlas and Gazetteer*, page 27.

Latitude: 36°39'22"N

Longitude: 118°18'37"W

Permits: None needed for day use; wilderness permit required for overnight stay.

Trailhead: Symmes Creek (Shepherd Pass trailhead). From Independence on Highway 395, go west on Market Street. After 4.5 miles, turn left on the unpaved Foothill Road. Follow signs to Shepherd Pass for 4.4 miles to the trailhead. Both Mount Williamson and neighboring Mount Tyndall are within the Bighorn Zoological Preserve, which is open to the public only from December 15 through July 15.

Mount Williamson

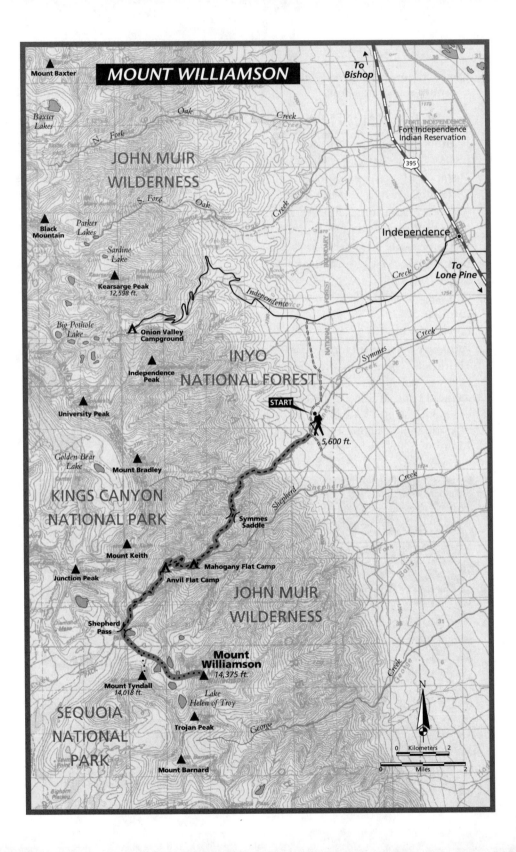

Mount Williamson is a large peak and a major undertaking. With almost 9,000 feet of vertical gain, a 15-mile trek to the peak, and exposed, Class 3 rock, it is not for the timid. The climb of Williamson is often combined with an ascent of Mount Tyndall on successive days.

From the trailhead, the route follows Symmes Creek for about a mile. Here the trail turns right (south) and begins a very steep (though shaded) switch-backed ascent to Symmes saddle, where you'll get the first fine view of Mount Williamson. It is good that this view is exhilarating, so you won't feel so badly when you have to lose 500 feet in elevation down to a long traverse. The traverse travels through open sagebrush country along a hillside to Shepherd Creek. From the creek, the trail rises back into the mountains and trees to a series of campgrounds. The first one is Mahogany Camp, not really far enough in for a serious Williamson–Tyndal base camp.

The first good overnight camp for climbing purposes is Anvil Camp, about 7 miles from the trailhead. Shepherd Pass is still well over 2 miles away, so early starts from Anvil are advised. Another solution is to camp at Shepherd Pass, or past it at one of the lakes in Williamson Bowl, depending on wilderness permits in effect at the time.

From Shepherd Pass hike southeast to Williamson Bowl, a large gravel basin west of the peak. Drop into this bowl, where there are four small lakes; the west-face route begins from the second lake. Climb the low-angle rock band above, aiming for the most prominent black watermark, and passing it on the right (south) side.

Above the watermark, climb the prominent chute that diagonals north. Exit the chute before rotten cliffs at the top by traversing right to a narrow slot. Ascend Class 3+ rock. From the top of this slot, it's an easy scramble to the summit plateau. A short stroll from here leads to the south (main) summit.

Retrace your route to descend; consider bringing a rope to rappel the Class 3 section.

44. MOUNT TYNDALL (NORTHWEST RIDGE)

Highlights: A dramatic peak with a sheer east face that drops thousands of feet from the summit to the talus below. It's a long hike, and for that reason, it's never crowded.

Distance: About 30 miles round trip (29 miles on trail, 1 mile off trail).

Difficulty: Class 2; strenuous.

Trailhead Elevation: 5,600 feet

Summit Elevation: 14,018 feet

Elevation Gain: 8,418 feet

Best Months: May to mid-July.

Maps: USGS Mount Williamson; DeLorme *Southern California Atlas and Gazetteer*, page 26.

Latitude: 37°06'35"N

Longitude: 118°29'30"W

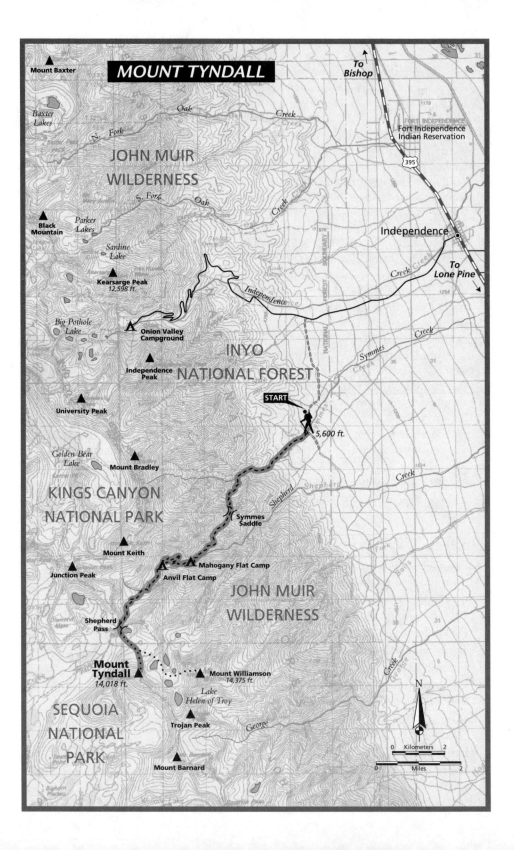

MOUNT TYNDALL

Mount Baxter

Baxter Lakes

JOHN MUIR WILDERNESS

Oak Creek

To Bishop

Fort Independence Indian Reservation

395

Independence

To Lone Pine

N. Fork

S. Fork

Oak Creek

Independence Creek

Black Mountain

Parker Lakes

Sardine Lake

Kearsarge Peak
12,598 ft.

Big Pothole Lake

Onion Valley Campground

INYO NATIONAL FOREST

Independence Creek

Symmes Creek

START

5,600 ft.

Independence Peak

University Peak

Shepherd Creek

Golden Bear Lake

Mount Bradley

Shepherd Creek

KINGS CANYON NATIONAL PARK

Symmes Saddle

Mount Keith

Mahogany Flat Camp

Junction Peak

Anvil Flat Camp

JOHN MUIR WILDERNESS

Diamond Mesa

Shepherd Pass

Bairs Creek

Mount Tyndall
14,018 ft.

Mount Williamson
14,375 ft.

Lake Helen of Troy

SEQUOIA NATIONAL PARK

Trojan Peak

George Creek

N

Mount Barnard

Kilometers 2

Miles 2

Bighorn Plateau

Permits: None needed for day use; wilderness permit required for overnight stay.
Trailhead: Symmes Creek (Shepherd Pass trailhead). From Independence on Highway 395, go west on Market Street. After 4.5 miles, turn left on the unpaved Foothill Road. Follow signs to Shepherd Pass for 4.4 miles to the trailhead. Both Mount Williamson and neighboring Mount Tyndall are within the Bighorn Zoological Preserve, which is open to the public only from December 15 through July 15.

The ascent of Mount Tyndall is a real workout, with more than 8,000 feet of vertical gain and a 15-mile hike to the peak. The climb of Tyndall is often combined with a climb of Mount Williamson on successive days (see Mount Williamson, climb #43).

From the trailhead, the route follows Symmes Creek for about a mile. Here the trail turns right (south) and begins a very steep (though shaded) switchbacked ascent to Symmes saddle. From the saddle, follow the route to Shepherd Creek and up the trail past Mahogany Camp. For your overnight campsite, continue on to Anvil Camp (about 7 miles from the trailhead) or to Shepherd Pass (2 miles farther), or even closer to Tyndall—depending on your wilderness permits.

From Shepherd Pass hike about a half-mile west (right) to the toe of Tyndall's prominent northwest ridge. Ascend this ridge, starting right of the rock rib. Pass through the notch at the top of the ridge. Scramble east up talus, ignoring the exposure to your left, to the summit

45. MOUNT WHITNEY

Highlights: Highest summit in the contiguous United States.
Distance:
   Main trail—21 miles round trip (all trail).
   Mountaineer's Route—15 miles round trip (about 10 miles on trail, about 5 miles of off-trail scrambling); or 18.5 miles as a loop, returning down the main trail.
Difficulty:
   Main trail—Class 1; strenuous.
   Mountaineer's Route—Class 3; strenuous.
Trailhead Elevation: 8,400 feet
Summit Elevation: 14,494 feet
Elevation Gain: 6,094 feet
Best Months: June through September.
Maps: USGS Mount Whitney; DeLorme *Southern California Atlas and Gazetteer*, page 27.
Latitude: 36°34'45"N
Longitude: 118°17'30"W
Permits: Daily quotas on the number of hikers hold year-round, but are more restrictive in prime summer months. Reservations for camping along the trail must be made in advance, as well as for staying overnight in the tiny stone cabin atop the summit. For more information, contact the Mount Whitney Ranger Station, P.O. Box 8, Lone Pine, CA 93545; (619) 876-6200;

Mount Whitney (left) and Split Mountain (back right)

www.r5.fs.fed.us/inyo/index.htm. Although the main Whitney Trail is subject to daily quotas, the Meysan Lake Trail and the North Fork of Lone Pine Creek are not, so the peaks on these approaches are possible alternatives if you get shut out on Whitney. (See Mount Russell, climb #47; Lone Pine Peak, climb #48; Mount LeConte, climb #49; Mount Mallory, climb #50; and Mount Irvine, climb #51.)

Trailhead: Whitney Portal. From Lone Pine on Highway 395, go west on Whitney Portal Road (at the only traffic light in Lone Pine) for 13 miles to Whitney Portal. The trailhead is on the right before the store; follow signs for parking options.

Get an early start. Rush hour here is at 4:00 A.M., when you can expect to find lines of hikers at the bathrooms. Rows of headlamps bobbing up the trail make for an unusual sight. Though you're almost always within sight or sound of other hikers as you move up the trail, the concentration of people per mile slowly thins out as each group finds its own pace.

The Mount Whitney Trail rises steadily right from the start as it begins the long ascent to the summit. At just under 1 mile it crosses the North Fork of Lone Pine Creek, and at 2.5 miles it crosses the South Fork. The trail ascends to the two approved camping areas along the route: Outpost Camp at 3.5 miles from the trailhead, and Trail Camp at 6 miles.

From there it's a tough 2 miles to Trail Crest, at 13,800 feet, where the trail enters Sequoia National Park. Half a mile farther, the Whitney Trail joins the John Muir Trail. Here the trail turns north up the Whitney massif, passing on the back side (west) of Mount Muir and Keeler Needle. The trail winds through an unending sea of white boulders. It always seems that there are more people in

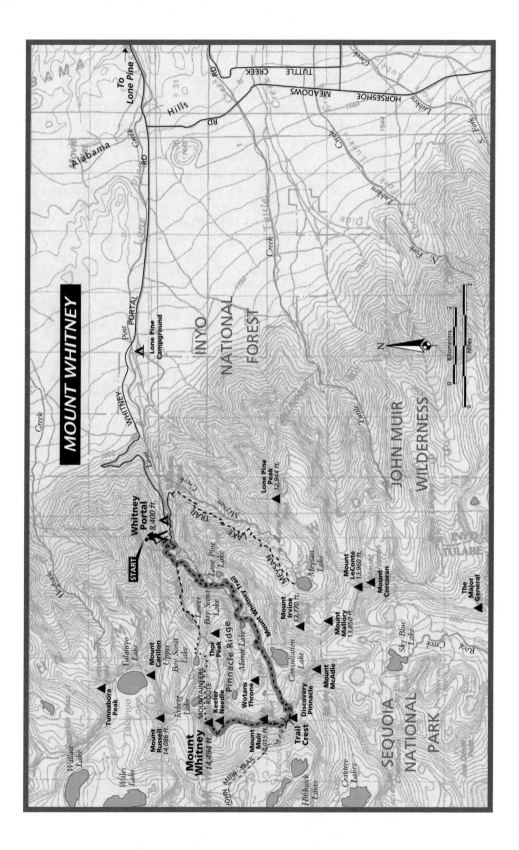

this area than on most of the earlier trail—perhaps it's the acclimatized turtles catching up with the lowland jackrabbits in this last section.

Finally, up switchbacks and through great fields of rock, you reach the summit of Mount Whitney. And if you are a slow hiker and get a late start back down the trail, take heart: The sunset over the Sierra is an awesome sight as well. Just make sure you carry plenty of extra flashlight batteries.

An alternative way up Whitney is via the Mountaineer's Route, a Class 3 (with careful routefinding) climb for people with mountaineering experience. First climbed by John Muir in 1873, the Mountaineer's Route ascends a gully just north of Mount Whitney and thus has a completely different approach, up the North Fork of Lone Pine Creek. Climbers on this route are not subject to the quotas imposed on the main trail.

For the Mountaineer's Route, hike up the main Whitney Trail for 1 mile to where it crosses the North Fork. This is usually the second place after the trailhead where water meets the trail, and the spot has been marked with a sign that indicates the North Fork, Lone Pine Creek. Find the rough trail that leaves the main trail here and continues up the south (left) side of the creek. This trail is steep and brush-filled.

Continue up the creek's canyon through trees and over boulders. When the canyon squeezes the trail out, cross the creek and head for the granite slab and wall on the other side known as the Ebersbacher Ledges. Follow the trail through tightly spaced trees. A useful landmark is a large, solitary foxtail pine—just look for the one tree that is three times as tall as any other. From here go right about 100 yards until the trail climbs and switchbacks to the left. The trail then leads up to Lower Boy Scout Lake (10,320), about 1.3 miles from the cutoff on the main Whitney Trail.

Cross to the south side of the creek and climb rocky slopes toward Upper Boy Scout Lake. At an obvious plateau the trail crosses to the north side of the creek and continues up wet slabs. Hike through Clyde Meadow to Upper Boy Scout Lake, at 11,300 feet, a little over a mile from Lower Boy Scout Lake. (The route to this point, Upper Boy Scout Lake, is identical to the approach for the ascent of Mount Russell.)

From Upper Boy Scout Lake, climb talus to the top of the ridge. Topping out on this ridge puts you below the majestic east faces of Keeler Needle, Day Needle, and Mount Whitney. Follow the trail west, then north, to Iceberg Lake, at 12,240 feet (and 5 miles from the Whitney Portal trailhead). The Mountaineer's Route proper starts in the gully just a short scramble above here. This is a good bivouac site.

To climb the route, enter the large and prominent gully above Iceberg Lake and just to the right of the Whitney summit. Ascend rocks, gravel, and small cliff bands, generally keeping to the right, toward the obvious slot above. Popping through the slot at an elevation of around 14,000 feet puts you at a point west of the summit. Continue west until an obvious, easy way to the summit appears on your left.

From the summit you have the choice of returning the way you came or descending the main trail. If you descend the Mountaineer's Route, be sure to hike several hundred yards west of Whitney's summit before beginning your descent to avoid technical terrain. (Head down about 75 yards northwest of the summit outhouse.) Some guides refer to the Mountaineer's Route as Class 4, allowing for the possible error of ending up in steeper terrain.

46. MOUNT MUIR
(VIA THE MOUNT WHITNEY TRAIL)

Highlights: A worthwhile side trip from the Mount Whitney Trail, giving you a sneak preview of the vertigo-inducing views to be savored on top of Whitney. Mount Muir is often climbed by those collecting ascents of 14,000-foot mountains.

Distance: About 17 miles round trip (16 miles on trail, less than a mile off trail).

Difficulty: Class 3; strenuous.

Trailhead Elevation: 8,400 feet

Summit Elevation: 14,015 feet

Elevation Gain: 5,615 feet

Best Months: June through September.

Maps: USGS Mount Whitney; DeLorme *Southern California Atlas and Gazetteer*, page 27.

Latitude: 36°33'50"N

Longitude: 118°17'28"W

Permits: Necessary. See permit information with Mount Whitney, climb #45.

Trailhead: Whitney Portal. From Lone Pine on Highway 395, go west on Whitney Portal Road for 13 miles to Whitney Portal. The trailhead is on the right, before the store.

Mount Muir is another 14,000-foot mountain along the Mount Whitney ridge. It is most often done as an add-on to a Whitney ascent day.

Follow the Whitney Trail (see Mount Whitney, climb #45) to the junction with the John Muir Trail just past Trail Crest. Mount Muir will appear on your right, just over a quarter-mile away. Scramble through boulders along a faint trail to the summit crag. The final ascent involves some Class 3 moves.

47. MOUNT RUSSELL

Highlights: An elegant fourteener featuring a long, exposed ridge, the longest in this guidebook. This fine ascent takes you away from the crowds on Mount Whitney.

Distance: About 12 miles round trip (almost all trail, with some sections of off-trail scrambling).

Difficulty: Class 3; strenuous.

Trailhead Elevation: 8,400 feet

Summit Elevation: 14,086 feet

Elevation Gain: 5,686 feet

Best Months: June through October.

Maps: USGS Mount Whitney; DeLorme *Southern California Atlas and Gazetteer*, page 27.

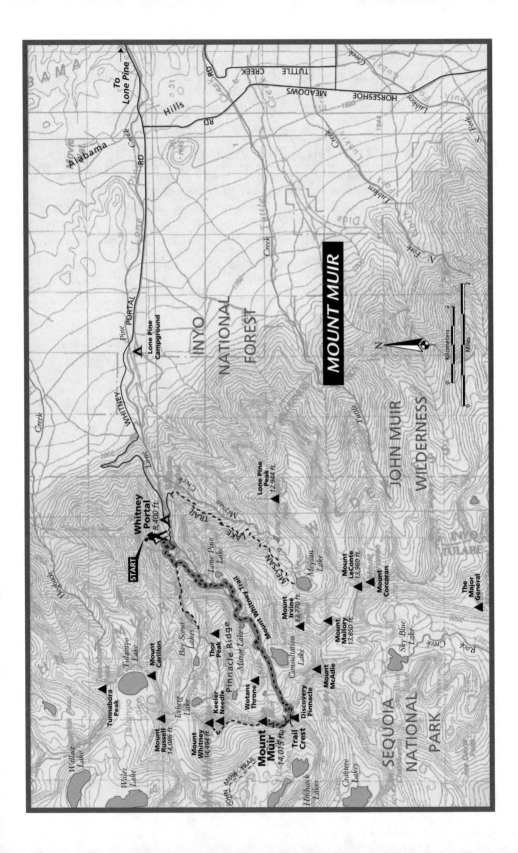

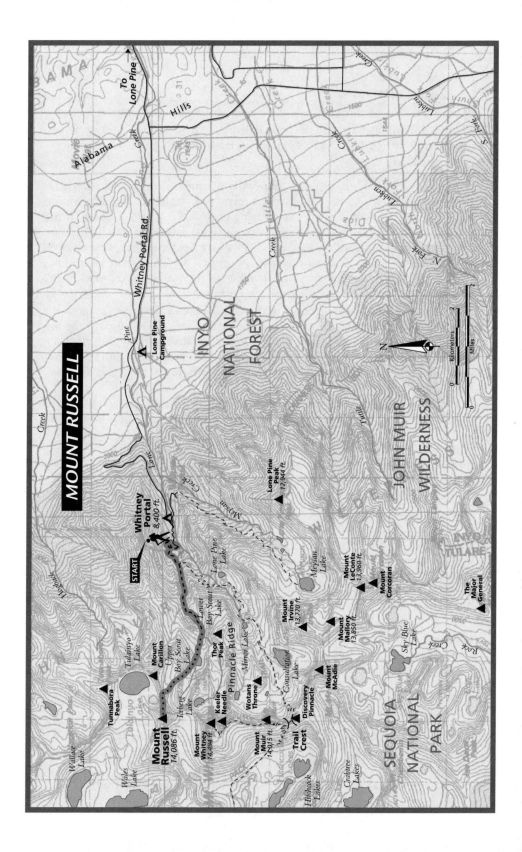

Latitude: 36°35'27"N
Longitude: 118°17'16"W
Permits: None needed for day use; wilderness permit required for overnight stay.
Trailhead: Whitney Portal. From Lone Pine on Highway 395, go west on Whitney Portal Road for 13 miles to Whitney Portal. The trailhead is on the right, before the store.

With its long ridge, Mount Russell dwarfs the Whitney massif in bulk, though it has to submit in height. Because of its geometry, many climbers consider Mount Russell to be the most aesthetically pleasing peak in the Whitney region. It has two summits, both over 14,000 feet, with the west one being the high point. Many technical routes adorn its flanks. The route described here, first climbed by Norman Clyde in 1926, is a classic ridge route. The penultimate section is a magnificent ascent up the east *arête* (ridge), with thousands of feet of exposure on either side. For all that, it is technically quite easy.

To ascend Mount Russell, start up the main Whitney Trail for 1 mile to the point where it crosses the North Fork of Lone Pine Creek. This is usually the second place after the trailhead where water meets the trail, and the spot has been marked with a sign that indicates the North Fork. Find the rough trail that leaves the main trail here and continues up the south (left) side of the creek. This trail is steep and brush-filled.

Continue up the creek's canyon through trees and over boulders. When the canyon squeezes the trail out, cross the creek and head for the granite slab and wall on the other side known as the Ebersbacher Ledges. Follow the trail through tightly spaced trees. A useful landmark is a large, solitary foxtail pine—just look for the one tree that is three times as tall as any other. From here go right about 100 yards until the trail climbs and switchbacks to the left. The trail then leads up to Lower Boy Scout Lake (10,320), about 1.3 miles from the cutoff on the main Whitney Trail.

Cross to the south side of the creek and climb rocky slopes toward Upper Boy Scout Lake. At an obvious plateau the trail crosses to the north side of the creek and continues up wet slabs. Hike through Clyde Meadow to Upper Boy Scout Lake, at 11,300 feet, a little over a mile from Lower Boy Scout Lake. (The route to this point, Upper Boy Scout Lake, is identical to the approach for the Mountaineer's Route up Mount Whitney.)

From Upper Boy Scout Lake, trek due east to an immense, gravelly incline heading northwest. This is the start of the southeastern end of Mount Russell. Ascend this incline to the saddle with the east *arête* (ridge). Follow the trail west along this *arête*, sometimes dropping to one side or the other of the actual crest, to the summit.

48. LONE PINE PEAK

Highlights: The best views of more peaks than from just about anywhere else in the Sierra. Long Pine Peak affords vistas that range from Mount Langley to Mount Russell and beyond.
Distance: About 11 miles round trip (6 miles on trail, 5 miles off trail).
Difficulty: Class 2; moderate/strenuous.

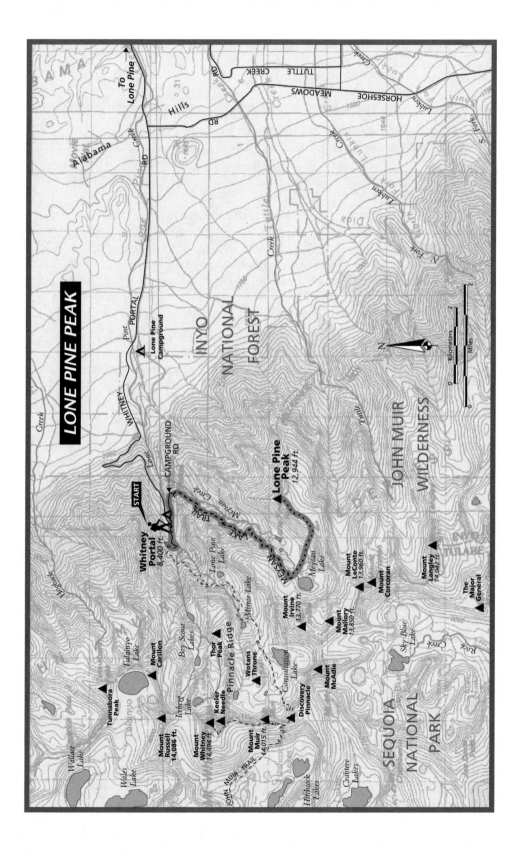

LONE PINE PEAK

Trailhead Elevation: 8,400 feet
Summit Elevation: 12,944 feet
Elevation Gain: 4,544 feet
Best Months: June through October or later, depending on the weather.
Maps: USGS Mount Langley; DeLorme *Southern California Atlas and Gazetteer*, page 27.
Latitude: 36°33'42"N
Longitude: 118°13'27"W
Permits: None needed for day use; wilderness permit required for overnight stay.
Trailhead: Whitney Portal, Meysan Lake Trail. From Lone Pine on Highway 395, go west on Whitney Portal Road for 13 miles to Whitney Portal. The Meysan Lake Trail starts from the lower Whitney Portal Campground. Walk along the campground loop road and follow the signs to the Meysan Lake trailhead. Once off the campground loop, follow signs past summer cottages, onto the trail on the north side of Meysan Creek.

Although the main Mount Whitney Trail is subject to daily use quotas year-round, the Meysan Lake Trail is not, so the peaks on this approach—Lone Pine, LeConte, Mallory, and Irvine—are possible alternatives if you get shut out on Whitney.

Lone Pine Peak is the formidable mountain that dominates the skyline from Lone Pine, and from Owens Valley in general. It is often assumed to be Mount Whitney. On its facets are several varied and challenging technical routes. The route described here is the easiest and shortest. What it lacks in aesthetics of ascent (much of the climb is a gravelly slog) it more than makes up for with the views from the summit.

From the trailhead, follow the signs for Meysan Lake. The trail to the lake is a pleasant 3-mile hike up a scenic valley. From Meysan Lake, follow the obvious chute northeast. Some of the slippery, troublesome scree can be avoided by climbing on the rock bands to the right. This, however, involves Class 3 climbing—even harder if you're not careful with routefinding. After attaining the summit plateau, walk northeast—through what must be the most false summits on any Sierra peak—to the one true summit.

At the top, you're popped into the center of an amazing cluster of peaks. The panorama sweeps from Mount Langley to Mount Russell, with close-ups of Mounts LeConte, Mallory, Irvine, Muir, and Whitney. From the summit you can pick out the climbing routes on Whitney and Keeler Needle. The photo opportunities are endless.

To descend, reverse your steps, then empty your shoes.

49. MOUNT LECONTE (NORTHWEST CHUTE)

Highlights: One member of an appealing threesome—LeConte, Mallory, and Irvine—gathered close together on a ridge above Meysan Lake. From Meysan Lake, LeConte is the left-most of the three peaks. From certain angles the ridge appears almost to be an infinite regression of spires disappearing to the south.
Distance: About 10 miles round trip (8 miles on trail, 2 miles off trail).
Difficulty: Class 3; moderate.

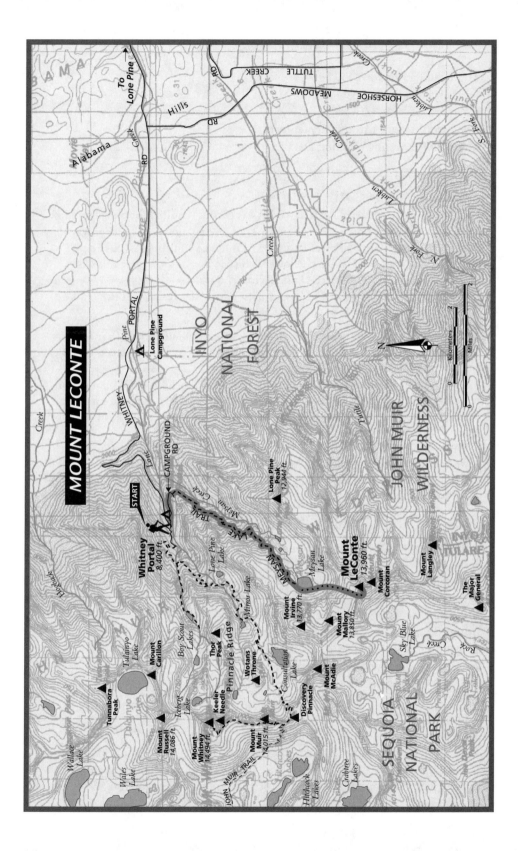

MOUNT LECONTE

Trailhead Elevation: 8,400 feet
Summit Elevation: 13,960 feet
Elevation Gain: 5,560 feet
Best Months: June through September.
Maps: USGS Mount Whitney; DeLorme *Southern California Atlas and Gazetteer*, page 27.
Latitude: 36°32'27"N
Longitude: 118°15'04"W
Permits: None needed for day use; wilderness permit required for overnight stay.
Trailhead: Whitney Portal, Meysan Lake Trail. From Lone Pine on Highway 395, go west on Whitney Portal Road for 13 miles to Whitney Portal. The Meysan Lake Trail starts from the lower Whitney Portal Campground. Walk along the campground loop road and follow the signs to the Meysan Lake trailhead. Once off the campground loop, follow signs past summer cottages, onto the trail on the north side of Meysan Creek.

Mount LeConte, along with its companions, Mounts Mallory and Irvine, can be accessed from Meysan Lake. The peaks make an attractive trio, tucked together into the highest part of the High Sierra.

From the trailhead, follow the signs for Meysan Lake, hiking for 3 miles along a pleasant trail up a scenic valley to the lake. From Meysan Lake follow a narrow, loose gully leading to a large cairn on the Mallory-LeConte plateau, at the base of LeConte's north face.

From here, drop down a slope and climb the prominent chute on the northwest side of Mount LeConte. A short Class 3 section known as the waterfall pitch, for obvious seasonal reasons, is passed near the summit. A short climb leads to the top of LeConte.

50. MOUNT MALLORY (EAST SLOPE)

Highlights: One of the challenging peaks on the same ridge with Mounts Irvine and LeConte.
Distance: About 9 miles round trip (7 miles on trail, 2 miles off trail).
Difficulty: Class 2; moderate.
Trailhead Elevation: 8,400 feet
Summit Elevation: 13,850 feet
Elevation Gain: 5,450 feet
Best Months: June through September.
Maps: USGS Mount Whitney; DeLorme *Southern California Atlas and Gazetteer*, page 27.
Latitude: 36°32'54"N
Longitude: 118°15'44"W
Permits: None needed for day use; wilderness permit required for overnight stay.
Trailhead: Whitney Portal, Meysan Lake Trail. From Lone Pine on Highway 395, go west on Whitney Portal Road for 13 miles to Whitney Portal. The Meysan Lake Trail starts from the lower Whitney Portal Campground. Walk

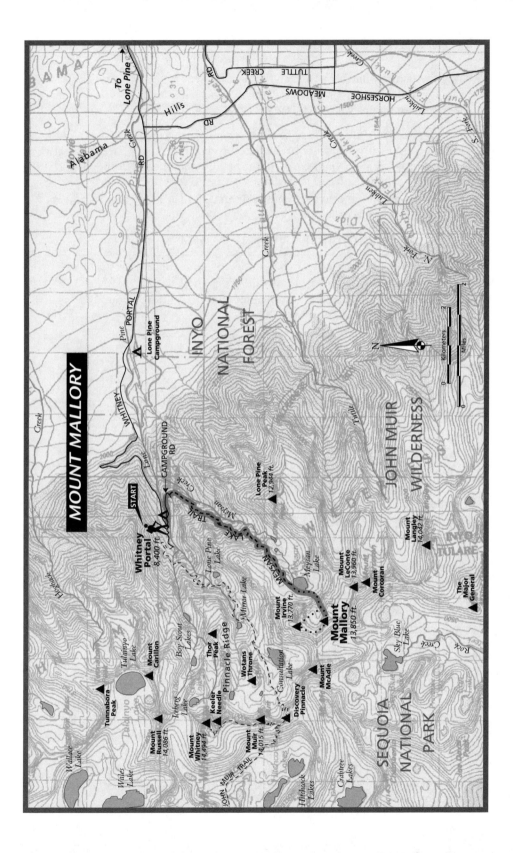

MOUNT MALLORY

START

Whitney
Portal
8,400 ft.

CAMPGROUND RD

Lone Pine
Campground

INYO

NATIONAL

FOREST

Lone Pine Peak
12,944 ft.

JOHN MUIR

WILDERNESS

Mount Langley
14,042 ft.

Mount LeConte
13,960 ft.

Mount Corcoran

The Major General

Mount Irvine
13,770 ft.

Mount Mallory
13,850 ft.

Mount McAdie

Discovery Pinnacle

Consultation Lake

Sky Blue Lake

Rock Creek

SEQUOIA

NATIONAL

PARK

Mount Muir
14,015 ft.

Mount Whitney
14,494 ft.

Keeler Needle

Mount Russell
14,086 ft.

Tunnabora Peak

Mount Carillon

Thor Peak

Pinnacle Ridge

Wotans Throne

Tulainyo Lake

Boy Scout Lakes

Mirror Lake

Lone Pine Lake

JOHN MUIR TRAIL

MT. WHITNEY TRAIL

MEYSAN

Meysan Lake

Meysan Creek

Lone Pine Creek

Whitney Portal Rd

To Lone Pine

Alabama

Hills

TUTTLE CREEK

HORSESHOE MEADOWS

Tuttle Creek

Lubken Creek

Diaz Creek

INYO TULARE

Crabtree Lakes

Hitchcock Lakes

Wales Lake

Wallace Lake

N

Kilometers

Miles

along the campground loop road and follow the signs to the Meysan Lake trail-head. Once off the campground loop, follow signs past summer cottages, onto the trail on the north side of Meysan Creek.

From the trailhead, follow the signs for Meysan Lake, hiking for 3 miles along a pleasant trail up a scenic valley to the lake. From Meysan Lake, ascend directly the obvious rocky slope to and up Mount Mallory. An alternate route is to tra-verse the ridge between Irvine and Mallory, a Class 3 route.

   The three adjoining peaks of Mallory, Irvine, and LeConte can all readily be climbed from Meysan Lake.

51. MOUNT IRVINE (EAST SLOPE)

Highlights: An alluring route up the prominent chute on the east side. Irvine shares a ridge with neighboring Mounts Mallory and LeConte.
Distance: About 9 miles round trip (6 miles on trail, 3 miles off trail).
Difficulty: Class 2; moderate.
Trailhead Elevation: 8,400 feet
Summit Elevation: 13,770 feet
Elevation Gain: 5,370 feet
Best Months: June through September.
Maps: USGS Mount Whitney; DeLorme *Southern California Atlas and Gazetteer,* page 27.
Latitude: 36°33'17"N
Longitude: 118°15'49"W
Permits: None needed for day use; wilderness permit required for overnight stay.
Trailhead: Whitney Portal, Meysan Lake Trail. From Lone Pine on Highway 395, go west on Whitney Portal Road for 13 miles to Whitney Portal. The Meysan Lake Trail starts from the lower Whitney Portal Campground. Walk along the campground loop road and follow the signs to the Meysan Lake trail-head. Once off the campground loop, follow signs past summer cottages, onto the trail on the north side of Meysan Creek.

From the trailhead, follow the signs for Meysan Lake, hiking for 3 miles along a pleasant trail up a scenic valley to the lake. From Meysan Lake, climb the chute that's just north of the east ridge of Mount Mallory. Where the chute ends, con-tinue west up the rocky slope (class 2) to the summit.

   The three adjoining peaks of Mallory, Irvine, and LeConte can all readily be climbed from Meysan Lake.

   There are two useful alternate routes up Mount Irvine. First, you can traverse to Irvine from Mount Mallory, following the ridge (Class 3). Or you can hike up from Arc Pass on the southwest side. This is a straightforward approach from the main Mount Whitney Trail (see Mount Whitney, climb #45). Leave the main trail just before Consultation Lake (about 3 miles from the Whitney Portal trailhead), following a use trail along the east shore, heading south toward Arc Pass, the low point on the ridge perpendicular to the Mallory/Irvine ridge. From Arc Pass, hike

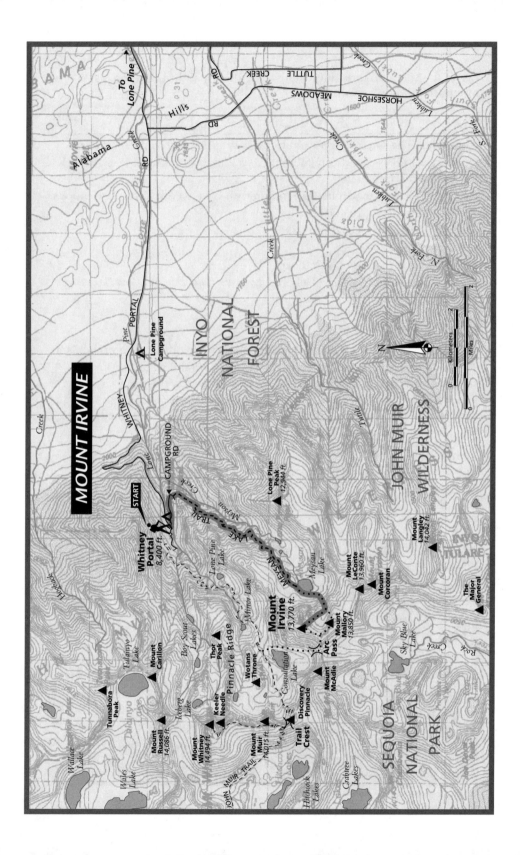

MOUNT IRVINE

START

Whitney
Portal
8,400 ft.

Lone Pine
Campground

To
Lone Pine →

Alabama

Hills

INYO

NATIONAL

FOREST

TUTTLE CREEK

HORSESHOE MEADOWS

JOHN MUIR

WILDERNESS

INYO
TULARE

Lone Pine Peak
12,944 ft.

Mount Langley
14,042 ft.

Mount LeConte
13,960 ft.

Mount Corcoran

The Major
General

Sky Blue
Lake

SEQUOIA

NATIONAL

PARK

Mount Irvine
13,770 ft.

Mount Mallory
13,850 ft.

Arc
Pass

Mount McAdie

Discovery
Pinnacle

Consultation
Lake

Wotans
Throne

Trail Crest

Mount Muir
14,015 ft.

Mount Whitney
14,494 ft.

Keeler
Needle

Pinnacle Ridge

Thor
Peak

Mount Carillon

Mount Russell
14,086 ft.

Tunnabora Peak

JOHN MUIR TRAIL

MAIN TRAIL

Meysan
Lake

Mirror Lake

Lone Pine Lake

Boy Scout
Lakes

Iceberg
Lake

Wales
Lake

Wallace
Lake

Tulainyo
Lake

Hitchcock
Lakes

Crabtree
Lakes

Rock Creek

east to the Mallory/Irvine ridge, descending slightly at the ridge, and just hike up Mount Irvine on the south slope.

52. MOUNT LANGLEY

Highlights: The southernmost California fourteener, with excellent views.

Distance: 21 miles round trip (all trail). As a linkup with Cirque Peak, 27 miles round trip (all trail).

Difficulty: Class 2; moderate. As a linkup with Cirque Peak, Class 2; strenuous.

Trailhead Elevation: 10,400 feet

Summit Elevation: 14,042 feet

Elevation Gain: 3,642 feet

Best Months: June through October.

Maps: USGS Mount Langley; DeLorme *Southern California Atlas and Gazetteer*, pages 27 and 39.

Latitude: 36°32'14"N

Longitude: 118°14'17"W

Permits: None needed for day use; wilderness permit required for overnight stay.

Trailhead: From Lone Pine, go west on Whitney Portal Road. After 3 miles, turn left (south) onto Horseshoe Meadows Road. Follow this road across the desert and up steep switchbacks for 22 miles to a complex of campgrounds and parking lots. Here, take the road branching right to the nearby signed trailhead for Cottonwood Lakes.

Mount Langley provides one of the most straightforward ascents of a Sierra fourteener. Though a long hike, the elevation gain is only a bit over 3,600 feet.

Mount Langley summit from the south

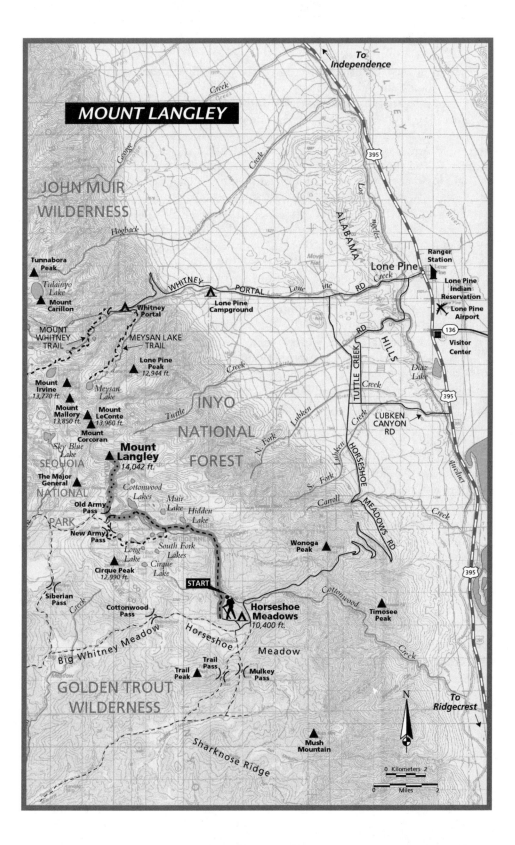

MOUNT LANGLEY

To Independence

JOHN MUIR WILDERNESS

Tunnabora Peak

Tulainyo Lake

Mount Carillon

WHITNEY PORTAL

Whitney Portal

Lone Pine Campground

Lone Pine

ALABAMA

Ranger Station

Lone Pine Indian Reservation

Lone Pine Airport

Visitor Center

MOUNT WHITNEY TRAIL

MEYSAN LAKE TRAIL

Lone Pine Peak 12,944 ft.

TUTTLE CREEK RD

HILLS

Diaz Lake

Mount Irvine 13,770 ft.

Meysan Lake

Mount Mallory 13,850 ft.

Mount LeConte 13,960 ft.

Mount Corcoran

INYO

NATIONAL

FOREST

LUBKEN CANYON RD

Sky Blue Lake

SEQUOIA

Mount Langley 14,042 ft.

The Major General

NATIONAL

Cottonwood Lakes

Muir Lake

Hidden Lake

Old Army Pass

PARK

New Army Pass

Long Lake

South Fork Lakes

Cirque Lake

Wonoga Peak

HORSESHOE MEADOWS RD

Cirque Peak 12,990 ft.

START

Siberian Pass

Cottonwood Pass

Horseshoe Meadows 10,400 ft.

Timosee Peak

Big Whitney Meadow

Horseshoe

Meadow

GOLDEN TROUT WILDERNESS

Trail Peak

Trail Pass

Mulkey Pass

N

To Ridgecrest

Sharknose Ridge

Mush Mountain

0 Kilometers 2

0 Miles 2

Follow the trail from the northwest end of the trailhead parking lot and hike 5 miles to Cottonwood Lakes.

From the lakes, Mount Langley looms to the north. From here the shortest route is via Old Army Pass. This pass, about 2 miles directly west of the lakes, is on an unmaintained trail, with sections that have been swept away. From the top of Old Army, steep scree leads north to Mount Langley. Hike to the summit plateau and continue to a dramatic cliff that drops off beneath your feet. Head right (east) at this point, circumnavigating the cliff bands to the summit.

You can also approach Langley via New Army Pass, a better trail, though it adds a mile to the ascent and an additional 700 feet in elevation gain. New Army Pass is reached by taking the trail to Long Lake; the cutoff to Long Lake is about 4.5 miles from the Cottonwood Lakes trailhead. Hike along this lake and you will see the lengthy switchbacked trail to New Army Pass.

To reach the summit of Langley from New Army Pass, hike north toward the mountain. First, drop 700 feet down, over scree and boulders, in 1 mile to a point just west of Old Army Pass. Continue to the top of Old Army Pass and then follow the route as described earlier in this section.

For the descent, most climbers favor the shorter route down from Old Army Pass to avoid additional elevation gain and to save time on the return.

The Mount Langley climb can be combined with Cirque Peak for a two-summit linkup (see Cirque Peak, climb #53).

53. CIRQUE PEAK

Highlights: An easily accessible peak with striking views, or a superlative peak linkup with Mount Langley.

Distance: 16 miles round trip (all trail). As a linkup with Mount Langley, 27 miles round trip (all trail).

Difficulty: Class 2; moderate. As a linkup with Mount Langley, Class 2; strenuous.

Trailhead Elevation: 10,400 feet

Summit Elevation: 12,990 feet

Elevation Gain: 2,590 feet

Best Months: June through September.

Maps: USGS Cirque Peak; DeLorme *Southern California Atlas and Gazetteer*, page 39.

Latitude: 36°23'87"N

Longitude: 118°14'10"W

Permits: None needed for day use; wilderness permit required for overnight stay.

Trailhead: From Lone Pine, go west on Whitney Portal Road. After 3 miles, turn left (south) onto Horseshoe Meadows Road. Follow this road across the desert and up steep switchbacks for 22 miles to a complex of campgrounds and parking lots. Here, take the road branching right to the nearby signed trailhead for Cottonwood Lakes.

Most hikers in this area are here to climb Mount Langley, a 14,000-foot peak. But nearby Cirque Peak also makes a worthy goal. It also can be part of a hiking or trail-running linkup with Langley.

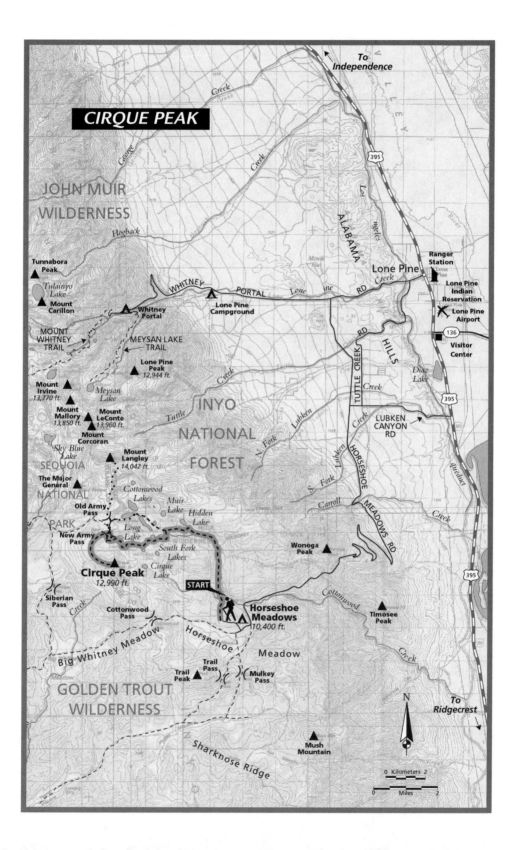

Cirque Peak

From the trailhead, follow the Cottonwood Lakes trail for about 4.5 miles, to the cutoff for the trail to Long Lake. This trail will take you along the shore of Long Lake and up a rocky grade to New Army Pass. Once on top of this long, rocky pass, the route to Cirque Peak to the south will be obvious. Circle around the long ridge bearing south and hike to the summit.

To complete a linkup with Mount Langley, first return to New Army Pass, then drop down to Old Army Pass. From Old Army, steep scree leads north to Langley. Hike to the summit plateau and continue to a dramatic cliff that drops off beneath your feet. Head right (east) at this point, circumnavigating the cliff bands to the summit (see Mount Langley, climb #52). The most efficient descent route is from Old Army Pass back down to Cottonwood Lakes, without returning to New Army Pass.

This two-summit adventure also makes one of the best long trail runs (marathon distance) in the Sierra.

54. OLANCHA PEAK

Highlights: The southernmost dramatic peak on the east side of the Sierra. Visible from Highway 395, the cliffs on the east face of Olancha Peak rise to a flat summit.

Distance: 13 miles round trip (all trail).

Difficulty: Class 3; strenuous.

Trailhead Elevation: 5,800 feet

Summit Elevation: 12,124 feet

Elevation Gain: 6,324 feet

Best Months: June through September.

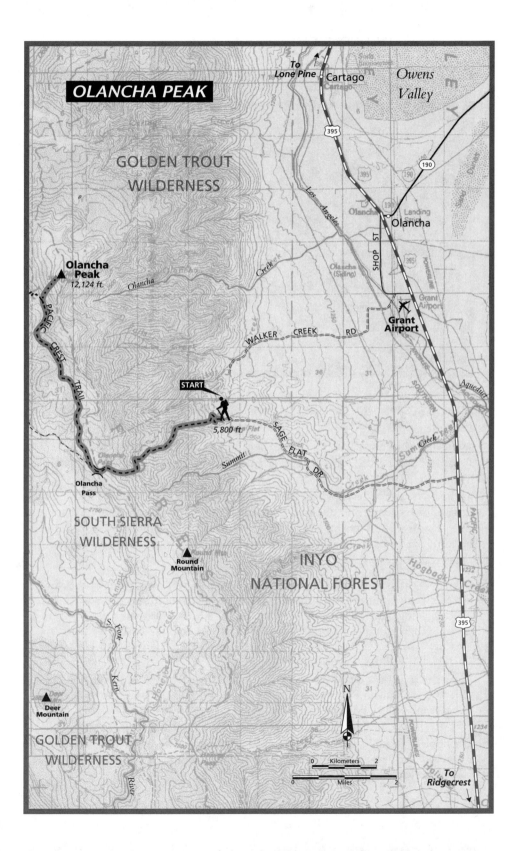

OLANCHA PEAK

GOLDEN TROUT
WILDERNESS

To
Lone Pine   Cartago

Owens
Valley

395

190

Olancha   190

Olancha

SHOP ST

Grant
Airport

Grant Airport

Olancha
Peak
12,124 ft.

Olancha

Olancha Creek

Creek

WALKER   CREEK   RD

PACIFIC CREST TRAIL

START

5,800 ft.

SAGE FLAT DR

Summit

Sum Creek

Olancha Pass

SOUTH SIERRA
WILDERNESS

Round
Mountain

INYO

NATIONAL FOREST

Hogback Creek

S. Fork

Deer
Mountain

N

395

GOLDEN TROUT
WILDERNESS

0   Kilometers   2

0   Miles   2

To
Ridgecrest

Olancha Peak

Maps: USGS Olancha; DeLorme *Southern California Atlas and Gazetteer*, page 39.
Latitude: 36°15'56"N
Longitude: 118°06'59"W
Permits: None needed for day use; wilderness permit required for overnight stay.
Trailhead: From Highway 395 at a point about 4 miles south of Olancha (just as the highway divides), go west on Sage Flat Drive. Follow the signs along this drive (which becomes an unpaved road) for about 6 miles to the trailhead. At this point is a public corral and an old ranch building. On the other side of the building is a fence and a trailhead sign for Olancha Peak. (Please don't park in the corral driveway.)

Olancha Peak is the prominent mountain rising above the ridgeline of the eastern Sierra south of the town of Olancha. Many references seem to regard this peak as being south of the High Sierra, but at 12,000 feet with a vertical gain of more than 6,000 feet from the trailhead, it will do. Like many of the lower-altitude east-Sierra trailheads, this one gets a lot of morning sun and heats up quickly. Early starts are desirable.

As the trail rises out of the sage and into the mixed conifer forest, the first objective is Olancha Pass, reached in 3.5 miles. Beyond the pass, the trail drops down from a rocky outcrop to a junction with the Pacific Crest Trail.

Take the Pacific Crest Trail north for a couple of miles as it rises up the western slope of Olancha Peak. Soon the foliage opens up and you get a good close-up view of the peak. Look for an obvious use trail heading east. Follow this steep, somewhat loose trail to the summit.

West of the Sierra Crest

Though the Sierra Nevada range is generally more dramatic from the east side, there are quality peaks on the western slope as well. The range rises more gradually on this side and is in a heavier precipitation zone, so the approaches are longer and tend to be more heavily forested. This section of the book covers several exceptions: climbs that are both enjoyable and readily accessible as day climbs.

Fresno Dome is a fun romp. Then, in the Mineral King area, several peaks can be reached from a road that bypasses many of the foothills. This road is an adventure in itself, and leads to an area that can hold its own with the rest of the Sierra.

55. FRESNO DOME

Highlights: An unlikely granite summit peering out of the pine and fir forest, with views of the Sierra and the San Joaquin Valley. The hike makes for a fine, short leg-stretcher, and the area offers good rock-climbing.

Distance: 1.6 miles round trip (all trail).

Difficulty: Class 1; easy.

Trailhead Elevation: 7,000 feet

Summit Elevation: 7,540 feet

Elevation Gain: 540 feet

Best Months: May through October.

Maps: USGS White Chief Mountain; DeLorme *Northern California Atlas and Gazetteer*, pages 120 and 121.

Latitude: 37°27'16"N

Longitude: 119°32'08"W

Permits: None needed.

Trailhead: Fifty-two miles north of Fresno (and 4 miles north of Oakhurst), on Highway 41, turn east on Road 632 (look for the big Sky Ranch Resort sign). Drive on this road for about 16 miles, following signs for Fresno Dome Campground. Staying on the main road, drive about a mile past the campground to a sign that says Fresno Dome Trailhead.

Fresno Dome is a pleasant diversion when driving south out of Yosemite, or for escaping the heat in Fresno, or as a warm-up for adventures to come. It's the easiest hike in this book. The dome is a great spot for a picnic, and it's an increasingly popular rock-climbing area.

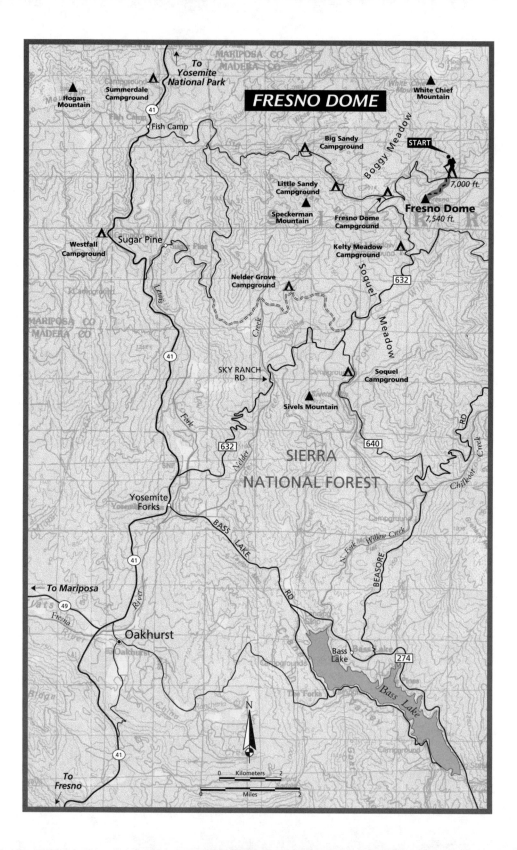

FRESNO DOME

To Yosemite National Park

Hogan Mountain

Summerdale Campground

41

Fish Camp

White Chief Mountain

Big Sandy Campground

Little Sandy Campground

Speckerman Mountain

START

7,000 ft.

Fresno Dome
7,540 ft.

Fresno Dome Campground

Westfall Campground

Sugar Pine

Kelty Meadow Campground

632

Nelder Grove Campground

Soquel Meadow

41

Lewis Fork

SKY RANCH RD →

Soquel Campground

Sivels Mountain

632

Nelder Creek

640

SIERRA

NATIONAL FOREST

Chilkoot Creek

RD

Yosemite Forks

BASS LAKE RD

N. Fork Willow Creek

BEASORE

To Mariposa

41

49

Fresno River

Oakhurst

Bass Lake

274

Bass Lake

To Fresno

41

MARIPOSA CO
MADERA CO

MARIPOSA CO
MADERA CO

Boggy Meadow

N

0   Kilometers   2

0   Miles   2

The trail starts in thick forest canopy and soon opens into a meadow. The trail becomes increasingly steep as it goes back into the trees, then opens onto an open rocky slope leading to the top.

56. SAWTOOTH PEAK

Highlights: A highly visible peak in a beautiful western Sierra setting, with views that cross the Sierra to Olancha Peak and Mount Langley as well as into Kings Canyon. The summit ridge resembles a serrated saw blade. The peak even has a perfect swimming lake, situated for a dip on the way down.

Distance: 12 miles round trip (all trail).

Difficulty: Class 2; moderate/strenuous.

Trailhead Elevation: 7,800 feet

Summit Elevation: 12,343 feet

Elevation Gain: 4,543 feet

Best Months: June through October.

Maps: USGS Mineral King; DeLorme *Southern California Atlas and Gazetteer*, page 38.

Latitude: 36°27'18"N

Longitude: 118°33'15"W

Permits: None needed for day use; wilderness permit required for overnight stay (available at the ranger station just before the trailhead).

Trailhead: From Visalia, take Highway 198 east to Three Rivers. Four miles east of Three Rivers is the well-marked start of Mineral King Road. This road is an adventure all on its own. Mostly paved, it winds for 25 miles up second-gear

Photo: U.S. Geological Survey/Matthes, F. E. 1154

Sawtooth Peak from the approach

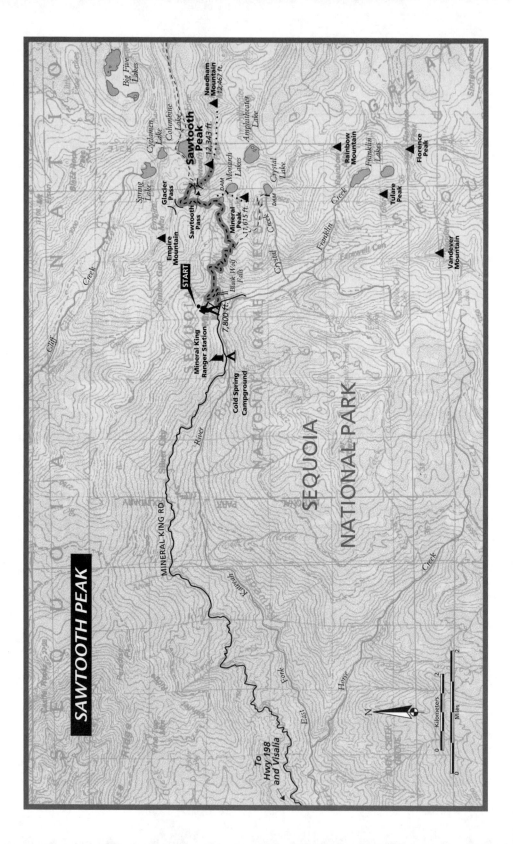

SAWTOOTH PEAK

Big Five
Lakes

Needham
Mountain
12,467 ft.

Sawtooth
Peak
12,343 ft.

Amphitheater
Lake

Cyclamen
Lake

Columbine
Lake

Rainbow
Mountain

Florence
Peak

Spring
Lake

Glacier
Pass

Monarch
Lakes

Crystal
Lake

Franklin
Lakes

Tulare
Peak

Empire
Mountain

Sawtooth
Pass

Mineral
Peak
11,615 ft.

Franklin Creek

Crystal Creek

Vandever
Mountain

START

Black Wolf
Falls

7,800 ft.

Mineral King
Ranger Station

Cold Spring
Campground

SEQUOIA NATIONAL GAME REFUGE

SEQUOIA

NATIONAL PARK

MINERAL KING RD

Kaweah River

East Fork

Horse Creek

To
Hwy 198
and Visalia

N

Kilometers

Miles

curves and grades. Giant sequoias (and huge stumps) appear intermittently along the road. Near the end, the sharp points of aptly named Sawtooth Peak incise the skyline. Camping is available a mile before the trailhead. The trail starts at the north end of the dirt parking lot on the left side of the road past some private cabins, and has a sign that indicates Sawtooth Pass.

Watch out for marmots at the Sawtooth Pass trailhead. They are large and ubiquitous; they chew on radiator hoses and fan belts and have been known to lodge themselves in engine compartments, causing damage and hitching rides. Check under your hood before leaving.

Study the excellent map on display at the trailhead parking lot for a preview of the route. From the trailhead, hike 4 miles—seemingly straight up; there's about 1,000 feet of elevation gain in the first nine-tenths of a mile. The route travels through thick pine and fir stands to a hillside that's open, except for a sparse stand of wind-sculpted foxtail pines, just below the first Monarch Lake.

From the lake (complete with sandy beach) you'll have an excellent view of the route up the peak from Sawtooth Pass. Take a dip in the lake now to clear your head for the hike up the pass or save it for washing off on the way down.

The trail gets a little confusing here; look for a Sawtooth Pass sign above the lake, hidden in boulders. (Do not go to the upper, dammed lake.) The trail from the first Monarch Lake to Sawmill Pass is a thankless 1.3-mile slog, but just when it seems like too much work, the majestic north face of Sawtooth Peak comes into view. From the pass, an obvious half-mile scramble puts you on top.

To reach the summit of neighboring Needham Mountain, just continue east for half a mile along the connecting ridge (see Needham Mountain, climb #57).

57. NEEDHAM MOUNTAIN

Highlights: A companion to and extension of Sawtooth Peak, with good views along much of the way.
Distance: 13 miles round trip (all trail).
Difficulty: Class 2; moderate/strenuous.
Trailhead Elevation: 7,800 feet
Summit Elevation: 12,467 feet
Elevation Gain: 4,667 feet
Best Months: June through October.
Maps: USGS Mineral King; DeLorme *Southern California Atlas and Gazetteer*, page 38.
Latitude: 36°27'15"N
Longitude: 118°32'11"W
Permits: None needed for day use; wilderness permit required for overnight stay (available at the ranger station just before the trailhead).
Trailhead: From Visalia, take Highway 198 east to Three Rivers. Four miles east of Three Rivers is the well-marked start of Mineral King Road. Mostly paved, it winds for 25 miles up second-gear curves and grades. Camping is available a mile before the trailhead. The trail starts at the north end of the dirt parking

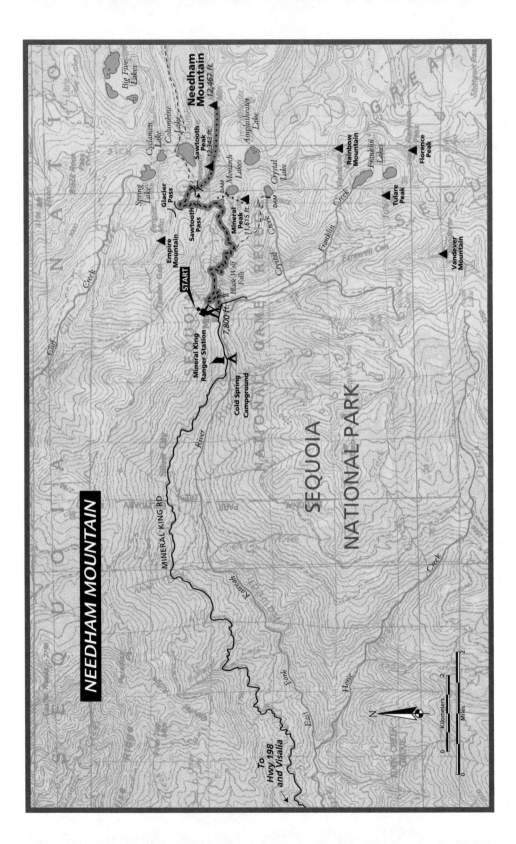

NEEDHAM MOUNTAIN

Big Five
Lakes

Needham
Mountain
12,467 ft.

Cyclamen
Lake

Columbine
Lake

Sawtooth
Peak
12,343 ft.

Amphitheater
Lake

Spring
Lake

Glacier
Pass

Rainbow
Mountain

Franklin
Lakes

Florence
Peak

Monarch
Lakes

Crystal
Lake

Sawtooth
Pass

DAM

Mineral
Peak
11,615 ft.

DAM

Tulare
Peak

Empire
Mountain

Crystal Creek

Franklin Creek

Eagle Lake

Vandever
Mountain

START

Black Wolf
Falls

7,800 ft.

Mineral King
Ranger Station

Cold Spring
Campground

MINERAL KING RD

River

Kaweah

SEQUOIA
NATIONAL PARK

NATIONAL GAME RESERVE

East Fork

Horse Creek

Creek

To
Hwy 198
and Visalia

N

Kilometers

Miles

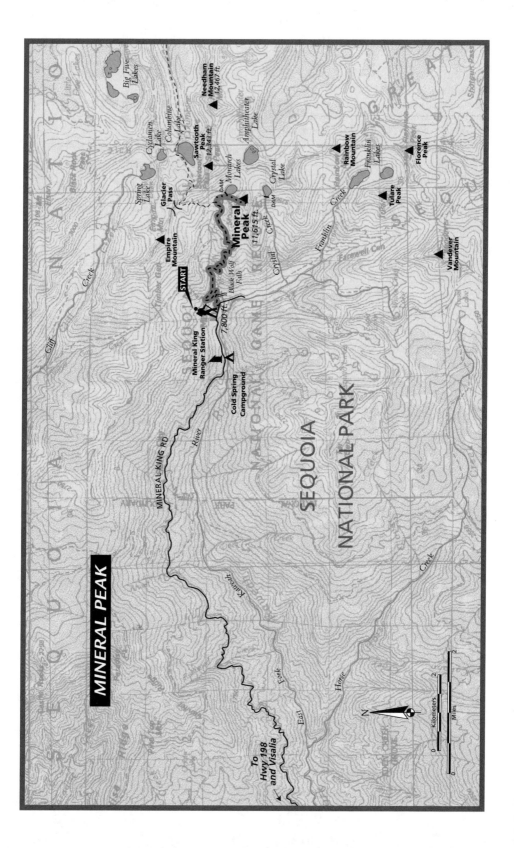

MINERAL PEAK

Needham Mountain 12,467 ft.

Sawtooth Peak 12,343 ft.

Big Five Lakes

Cyclamen Lake

Columbine Lake

Spring Lake

Glacier Pass

Empire Mountain

Amphitheater Lake

Monarch Lakes

Crystal Lake

Rainbow Mountain

Florence Peak

Franklin Lakes

Tulare Peak

DAM

Mineral Peak 11,615 ft.

START

Black Wolf Falls

7,800 ft.

Mineral King Ranger Station

Franklin Creek

Crystal Creek

Farewell Can.

Vandever Mountain

Cold Spring Campground

MINERAL-KING RD

Kaweah

River

East Fork

Horse Creek

To Hwy 198 and Visalia

SEQUOIA
NATIONAL PARK

SEQUOIA   NATIONAL   GAME   REFUGE

N

Kilometers   0   2

Miles   0   2

lot on the left side of the road past some private cabins, and has a sign that indicates Sawtooth Pass.

At the trailhead, watch out for marmots, which have been known to get into vehicle engine compartments and chew on radiator hoses and fan belts.

The trail to Needham Mountain crosses over the summit of Sawtooth Peak, so the routes to the two peaks are identical except at the very end (see Sawtooth Peak, climb #56). From the top of Sawtooth Peak, continue east along its summit ridge. Stay below and south of the pinnacles on the ridge for the half-mile walk from Sawtooth to the summit of Needham.

58. MINERAL PEAK

Highlights: An abrupt and photogenic peak with great views.

Distance: 12 miles round trip (9 miles on trail, 3 miles off trail).

Difficulty: Class 2; moderate/strenuous.

Trailhead Elevation: 7,800 feet

Summit Elevation: 11,615 feet

Elevation Gain: 3,815 feet

Best Months: June through October.

Maps: USGS Mineral King; DeLorme *Southern California Atlas and Gazetteer*, page 38.

Latitude: 36°26'48"N

Longitude: 118°33'49"W

Permits: None needed for day use; wilderness permit required for overnight stay (available at the ranger station just before the trailhead).

Trailhead: From Visalia, take Highway 198 east to Three Rivers. Four miles east of Three Rivers is the well-marked start of Mineral King Road. Mostly paved, it winds for 25 miles up second-gear curves and grades. Camping is available a mile before the trailhead. The trail starts at the north end of the dirt parking lot on the left side of the road past some private cabins, and has a sign that indicates Sawtooth Pass.

Mineral Peak is the strikingly foreboding-looking peak rising just south of the Monarch Lakes. From the trailhead, hike 4.5 miles to the first Monarch Lake. From the lake, strike out to the south, up a good use trail at first, then pure cross-country. Head up the ridge through sage and low brush toward the obvious summit.

About three-quarters of the way from the lake, the topography becomes steep, and an intimidating rock headwall looms ahead. Have no fear, there is a way: Traverse around to the right (south), where steep scrambling leads up easy terrain to the summit block.

White Mountains and Death Valley

East of the Sierra, across Owens Valley, is the start of the basin and range province, a geographic and geologic region stretching east across Nevada to the Wasatch Mountains of Utah. This a land of alternating desert mountain ranges and deep valley basins.

The White Mountains are the first of these ranges. Though a lot smaller in extent and generally not as high as the Sierra, this is a significant range. The highest point, White Mountain Peak, at 14,246 feet, is the third-highest in California (after Mount Whitney and Mount Williamson).

Death Valley is the lowest of the intermountain valleys. It is flanked on its west by the Panamint Range, which contains Wildrose and Telescope Peaks. Telescope Peak is the high point of the Panamints, as well as of Death Valley National Park. Waucoba Mountain is the high point of the Inyo Mountains, a range that lies between the White Mountains and the Panamints.

59. WHITE MOUNTAIN PEAK

Highlights: Highest summit in the White Mountains, and the third-highest peak in California. It also offers the easiest ascent of any of California's 14,000-foot mountains.

Distance: 14 miles round trip (all trail).

Difficulty: Class 2; moderate.

Trailhead Elevation: 12,000 feet

Summit Elevation: 14,246 feet

Elevation Gain: 2,246 feet

Best Months: July through September, depending on snow.

Maps: USGS White Mountain Peak; DeLorme *Northern California Atlas and Gazetteer*, pages 113, 114, 123, 124.

Latitude: 37°38'04"N

Longitude: 118°15'17"W

Permits: None needed for day use; wilderness permit required for overnight stay (available at the ranger station just before the trailhead).

Trailhead: From the town of Big Pine, 14 miles south of Bishop on Highway 395, turn east on Highway 168. After 12.5 miles, turn north on White Mountain Road. After 11 miles you'll reach the Schulman Grove Visitor Center and

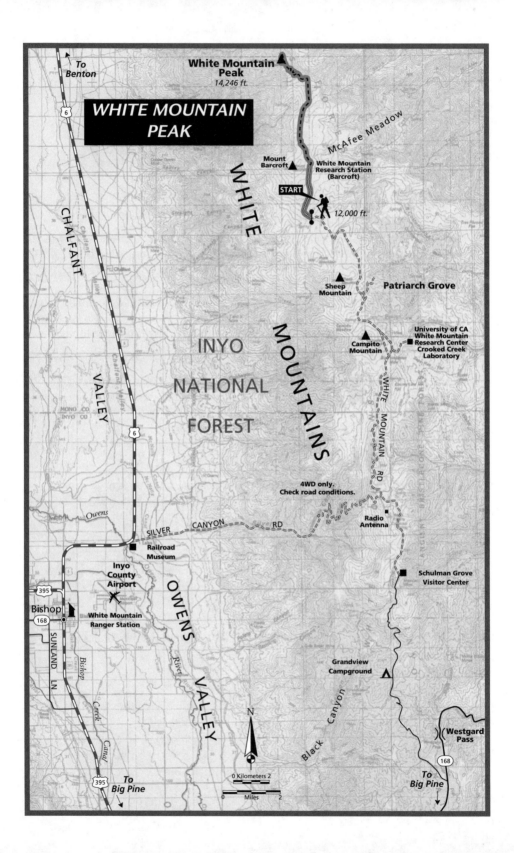

White Mountain Peak

the Schulman Grove of ancient bristlecone pines. Shortly after the center, the paved road turns to dirt. Follow signs for the Patriarch Grove, situated about 10.5 miles beyond Schulman Grove. Five miles later you'll arrive at a locked gate across the road, marking the trailhead.

The trail starts high, at an elevation of 12,000 feet, so the 7-mile route to the summit has only a gradual grade. From the trailhead, the route follows an old access road that, after 2 miles, leads to the University of California's White Mountain Research Station (generally know by its older name, Barcroft).

After the research station, the trail crests a pass. The way to the summit is visible from the pass. Austere, windswept rock formations punctuate the rolling plain. The trail descends abruptly before the final grade, where it then switchbacks up scree to the summit. There are more research facilities on the summit. From here you'll be looking out over Death Valley to the south and Nevada's basin and range topography to the east. To the west stands the abrupt eastern rampart of the Sierra Nevada—the best panoramic view of the Sierra, period.

60. WAUCOBA MOUNTAIN

Highlights: Highest peak in the Inyo Mountains—a gentle, rounded summit perfect for a moderate climb.

Distance: 6 miles round trip (all trail). As a loop hike including the summit of Squaw Peak, 9 miles total (all trail).

Difficulty: Class 2; moderate.

Trailhead Elevation: 8,000 feet

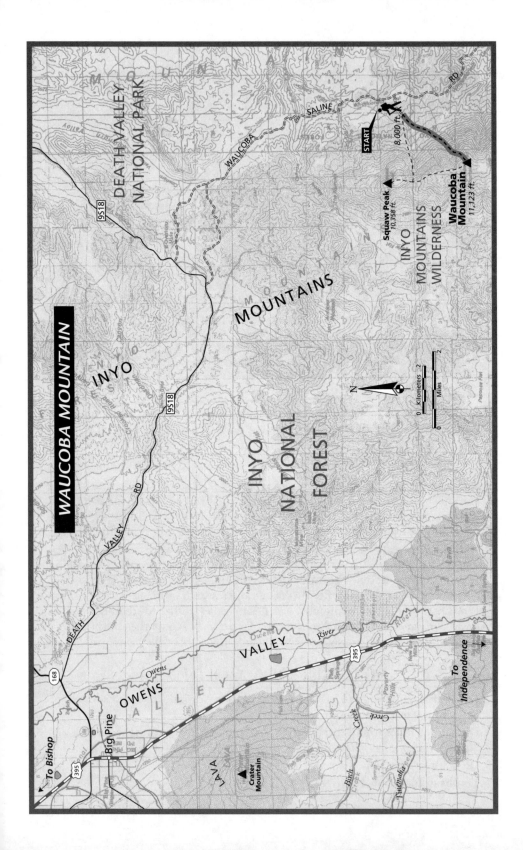

Waucoba Mountain (left) and Squaw Peak (right)

Summit Elevation: 11,123 feet

Elevation Gain: 3,123 feet

Best Months: May through November.

Maps: USGS Waucoba Mountain; USGS Waucoba Spring; DeLorme *Northern California Atlas and Gazetteer*, page 124.

Latitude: 37°01'20"N

Longitude: 118°00'23"W

Permits: None needed for day use; wilderness permit required for overnight stay (available in Death Valley or Big Pine).

Trailhead: From Big Pine on Highway 395, travel east on Highway 168 for 2.5 miles to Death Valley Road (Forest Service Road 9S18). Follow Death Valley Road for 13 miles to Waucoba Saline Road—a good dirt road on the right, marked with a sign. Take this road, also for 13 miles, to a faint dirt road on the right (west) below Waucoba Mountain and Squaw Peak. Follow the road a short distance to its end.

From the trailhead, follow an old track southwest through piñon pines to Waucoba Mountain's open northwest slope. Follow this track to the summit.

You can make this a loop hike that includes neighboring Squaw Peak by continuing north from the Waucoba summit along the ridgeline to the Waucoba–Squaw saddle and then on to the summit of Squaw Peak. To complete the loop, follow the trail that leads east-southeast from the summit of Squaw back to the trailhead.

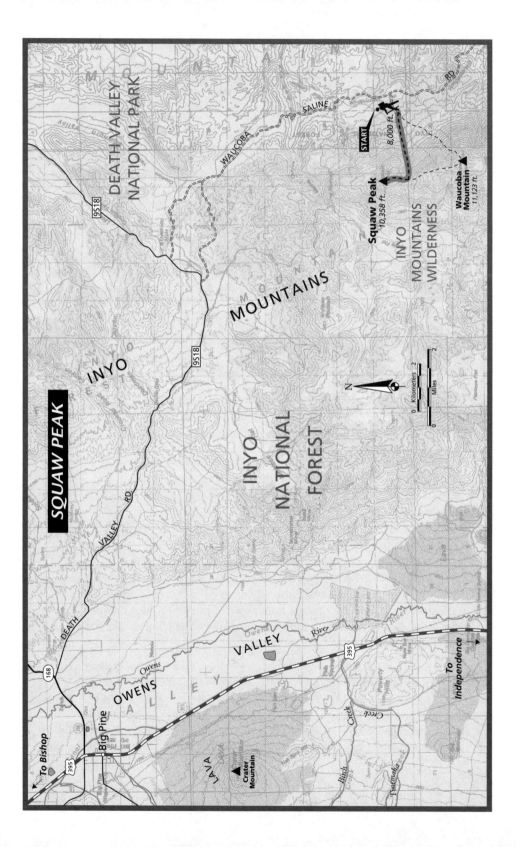

61. SQUAW PEAK

Highlights: Spectacular views of Death Valley, Owens Valley, and the eastern Sierra. A pleasant loop hike when combined with an ascent of neighboring Waucoba Mountain.

Distance: 4 miles round trip (all trail). As a loop hike including the summit of Waucoba Mountain, 9 miles total (all trail).

Difficulty: Class 2; moderate.

Trailhead Elevation: 8,000 feet

Summit Elevation: 10,358 feet

Elevation Gain: 2,358 feet

Best Months: May through November.

Maps: USGS Waucoba Mountain; USGS Waucoba Spring; DeLorme *Northern California Atlas and Gazetteer*, page 124.

Latitude: 37°03′10″N

Longitude: 118°00′55″W

Permits: None needed for day use; wilderness permit required for overnight stay (available in Death Valley or Big Pine).

Trailhead: From Big Pine travel east on Highway 168, 2.5 miles to Death Valley Road (Forest Service Road 9S18). Follow this for 13 miles to the Saline Valley Road, a good dirt road on the right marked with a sign. Follow the Waucoba Saline Road for another 13 miles to a faint dirt road on the right (west) below Waucoba Mountain and Squaw Peak. Follow this a short distance to its end.

From the trailhead, hike northwest along a faint use trail through piñon pines to the Waucoba/Squaw Peak saddle. Here the trail joins the one from Waucoba Mountain. In spring, after the snow melts, there are desert wildflowers and flowering cacti here. Follow the ridge to the summit of Squaw Peak.

To make this a loop hike that includes neighboring Waucoba Mountain, follow the ridge south to the Waucoba–Squaw saddle and then on to the summit of Waucoba. To complete the loop, follow the old track that leads northeast from the summit of Waucoba back to the trailhead.

62. WILDROSE PEAK

Highlights: An easy hike from a remote trailhead, offering views of the Panamints, the Sierra, and Death Valley. Desert wildflowers and flowering cacti may also be seen.

Distance: 8.4 miles round trip (all trail).

Difficulty: Class 2; moderate.

Trailhead Elevation: 6,900 feet

Summit Elevation: 9,064 feet

Elevation Gain: 2,164 feet

Best Months: April through November, later depending on snow conditions.

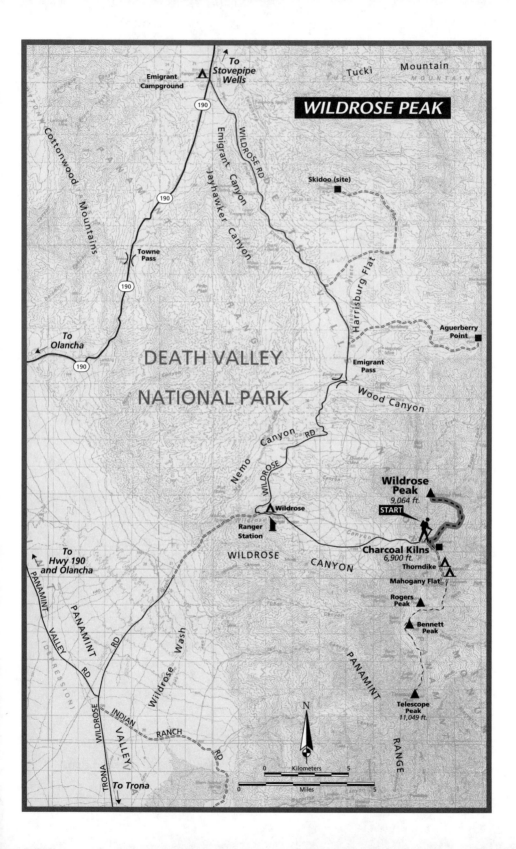

WILDROSE PEAK

To Stovepipe Wells
Emigrant Campground
190
Tucki Mountain

Cottonwood Mountains
PANAMINT
Emigrant Canyon
Jayhawker Canyon
WILDROSE RD

Skidoo (site)

190

190
Towne Pass

190
To Olancha

DEATH VALLEY
NATIONAL PARK

Harrisburg Flat

Aguerberry Point

Emigrant Pass

Wood Canyon

Nemo Canyon
Canyon RD
WILDROSE

Wildrose Peak
9,064 ft.
START

Wildrose
Ranger Station

WILDROSE
CANYON

Charcoal Kilns
6,900 ft.
Thorndike
Mahogany Flat

To Hwy 190 and Olancha

PANAMINT VALLEY
RD

Rogers Peak

Bennett Peak

Wildrose Wash
(DEPRESSION)
PANAMINT VALLEY

WILDROSE RD

INDIAN VALLEY
RANCH RD

TRONA

To Trona

PANAMINT RANGE

Telescope Peak
11,049 ft.

N

0   Kilometers   5
0   Miles   5

Charcoal kilns, Wildrose Peak trailhead

Maps: USGS Wildrose Peak; DeLorme *Southern California Atlas and Gazetteer*, page 41.
Latitude: 36°16′33″N
Longitude: 117°04′41″W
Permits: None needed for day use; wilderness permit required for overnight stay.
Trailhead: Charcoal kilns. From Olancha on Highway 395, take Highway 190 east past Keeler and Darwin for 52 miles to Wildrose Road, within a few miles of Stovepipe Wells. Turn south on Wildrose and take the road for 26 miles to the charcoal kilns. You can also get to the charcoal kilns from the south, via the Trona Wildrose Road from the town of Trona. It's about 45 miles from Trona to the charcoal kilns; stay right at the junction with Panamint Valley Road, and follow the signs to the kilns. The trail starts from the west end of the charcoal kilns.

The charcoal kilns are fascinating structures and worth tarrying for. At one time this area was denuded of trees to produce charcoal. When it became impractical to transport wood here any longer, the operation moved on and the kilns were abandoned. The site has interpretive signs that tell about their history and function.

Follow the trail as it climbs through piñon pines, Utah junipers, and cactus, often with wildflowers (Indian paintbrush and several varieties of lupine) on display. You'll reach a shoulder after 1.8 miles that begins to provide views down into Death Valley. Three miles into the hike, from a plateau, you'll see the summit ahead. This last section is steep but short. The summit is open, the view panoramic.

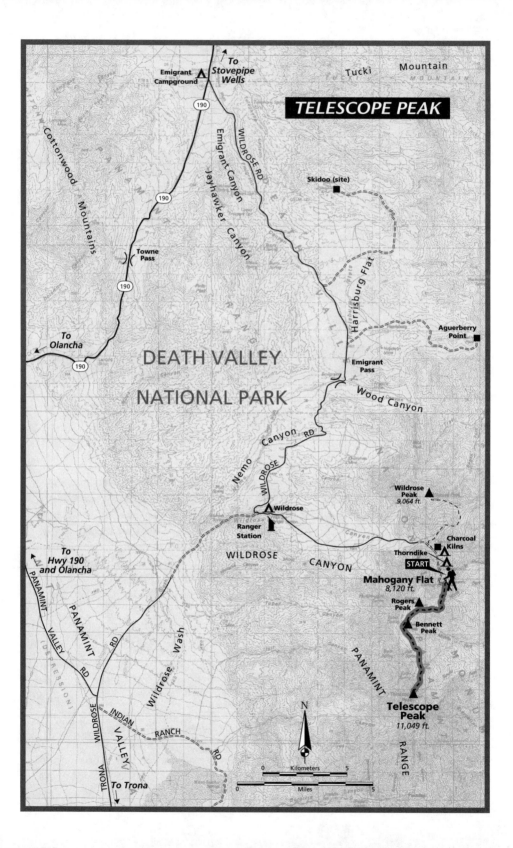

TELESCOPE PEAK

To *Stovepipe Wells*

Emigrant Campground

190

Tucki   Mountain

TUCKI   MOUNTAIN

Cottonwood   Mountains

Emigrant Canyon

Jayhawker Canyon

WILDROSE RD

190

Skidoo (site)

Towne Pass

190

To *Olancha*

190

DEATH VALLEY

NATIONAL PARK

Harrisburg Flat

Aguerberry Point

Emigrant Pass

Wood Canyon

Nemo Canyon

Canyon RD

WILDROSE

Wildrose

Ranger Station

WILDROSE   CANYON

Wildrose Canyon

Wildrose Peak
9,064 ft.

Charcoal Kilns

Thorndike

START

Mahogany Flat
8,120 ft.

Rogers Peak

Bennett Peak

To *Hwy 190 and Olancha*

PANAMINT VALLEY (DEPRESSION)

PANAMINT RD

Wildrose Wash

PANAMINT   RANGE

Telescope Peak
11,049 ft.

INDIAN   RANCH   RD

VALLEY

WILDROSE RD

TRONA

To *Trona*

N

Kilometers
0   5

Miles
0   5

Telescope Peak

63. TELESCOPE PEAK

Highlights: Highest point in Death Valley National Park. It offers wildflowers—and great views of the Panamints, Sierra Nevada, and Death Valley.

Distance: 14 miles round trip (all trail).

Difficulty: Class 2; moderate/strenuous.

Trailhead Elevation: 8,120 feet

Summit Elevation: 11,049 feet

Elevation Gain: 2,929 feet

Best Months: April through November, depending on snow conditions.

Maps: USGS Telescope Peak; Delorme *Southern California Atlas and Gazetteer*, page 41.

Latitude: 36°10'11"N

Longitude: 117°05'16"W

Permits: None needed for day use; wilderness permit required for overnight stay.

Trailhead: Mahogany Flat Campground. From Olancha on Highway 395, take Highway 190 east for 52 miles to Wildrose Road, within a few miles of Stovepipe Wells. Turn south on Wildrose and take the road for 27.6 miles, past the charcoal kilns, to Mahogany Flat Campground. The last 1.5 miles from the charcoal kilns to Mahogany Flat are over a steep road of loose gravel and rock, passable with two-wheel drive and attitude (has been done in a low-slung Swedish sports sedan, but the car was never the same again). You can also get to Mahogany Flat from the south, via the Trona Wildrose Road from the town of Trona. It's about 46.5 miles from Trona to Mahogany Flat; stay right at the junction with Panamint Springs Road, and follow the signs to the charcoal kilns and then Mahogany Flat.

The only thing better than watching the sun set behind Telescope Peak from the hot pool at Furnace Creek is looking at that scene knowing that you stood on the summit just a short while ago. This is a hike of contrasts, winding and revealing different terrain as you go, the expanse of Death Valley visible the whole way.

From the trailhead at Mahogany Flat, hike out of the campground in a piñon forest, past a locked gate. Wind around Rogers Peak to Arcane Meadows, a distance of about 2.3 miles. Like the hike as a whole, this is a straightforward route. Take advantage of the western views, but don't be surprised if this open section, especially just past Bennett Peak, is very windy.

Shortly before the final grade to the summit, you'll enter a forest of bristlecone and limber pines. You'll see wonderful examples of wood sculpted by wind and sand. The trail dips down here, then up again to follow a narrow ridge to the summit.

Southern California

A series of mountain ranges south of the Sierra Nevada offer a number of worthy summits. The ranges represented in this book are the San Jacinto, San Gorgonio, San Gabriel, and Mojave.

The San Jacinto Mountains stretch from outside of Palm Springs up to the summit of San Jacinto Peak at almost 11,000 feet. Every climatic zone from desert to alpine is represented. The San Gorgonio Mountains start higher and are more consistently wooded. The San Gabriels are also wooded and temperate, but are most noted for the way they rise directly out of Los Angeles. The Mojave is a pure desert mountain range.

64. MOUNT BADEN-POWELL

Highlights: A charming hike, and a great warm-up peak. The mountain, honoring the founder of the Boy Scouts, is an excellent hike for scouts of all ages.
Distance: 8 miles round trip (all trail).
Difficulty: Class 2; easy.
Trailhead Elevation: 6,556 feet
Summit Elevation: 9,399 feet
Elevation Gain: 2,843 feet
Best Months: May through September.
Maps: USGS Crystal Lake; Delorme *Southern California Atlas and Gazetteer*, page 94; Tom Harrison, Angeles High Country.
Latitude: 34°17'20"N
Longitude: 117°38'45"W
Permits: None needed for day use; wilderness permit required for overnight stay (available at the ranger station a few miles before the trailhead). In addition, a pass (Adventure Pass) is necessary for parking (available at state and federal ranger stations).
Trailhead: Mount Baden-Powell trailhead, Vincent Gap parking area. From the west, starting from Burbank, drive 3 miles south on Interstate 5 to Highway 134 in Glendale, and take this route 3 miles east to Highway 2. Travel on Highway 2 for 58 miles, passing La Canada, to the trailhead. From the east, take the Wrightwood exit off I–15, 3 miles south of Cajon Pass, and travel 8 miles west on Highway 138 to the intersection with Highway 2. From here travel 14 miles west to the trailhead (an almost complete view of the route is seen from this approach). The signed trailhead includes a parking lot on the south side of the highway, at the base of the mountain.

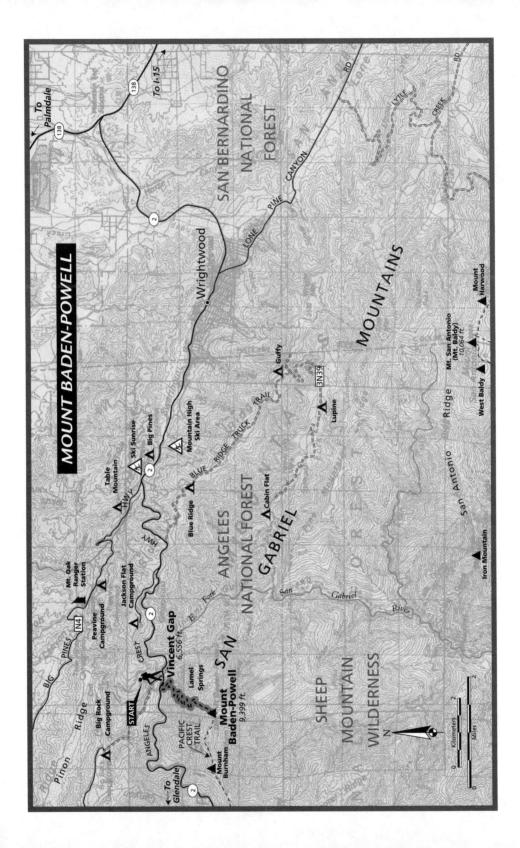

MOUNT BADEN-POWELL

Mount Baden-Powell

This is a very straightforward trail. From the trailhead, ascend switchbacks through a mixed conifer forest along the northeast-facing slope of the mountain, up the Vincent Gulch divide. After 1.5 miles, a short spur trail offers a side trip to Lamel Springs, a shaded spring 100 yards off the main trail. The main trail, shortly before the summit, enters a stand of weathered limber pines; a side trail from here leads an eighth of a mile into the heart of this thicket. The trees' gnarled appearance is reminiscent of the Schulman Grove of bristlecones in the White Mountains.

A short distance beyond the limber pines, you'll arrive at the open summit. Look for ladybug swarms in the spring. At the summit is a monument to Baden-Powell. Do you know the twelve things a Scout is? If not, you'll have to read the plaque.

From the summit you can see all over the southland, including Mount San Antonio, San Gorgonio Mountain, and San Jacinto Peak.

65. MOUNT SAN ANTONIO (MOUNT BALDY)

Highlights: A great escape from the noise and crowds of Los Angeles, minutes from downtown. This loop hike takes you from the desert into pine forest. The summit is the high point of the San Gabriel Mountains.

Distance: 11-mile loop (all trail).

Difficulty: Class 2; strenuous.

Trailhead Elevation: 6,264 feet

Summit Elevation: 10,064 feet

Elevation Gain: 3,800 feet

Best Months: April through November; may be too hot in midsummer.

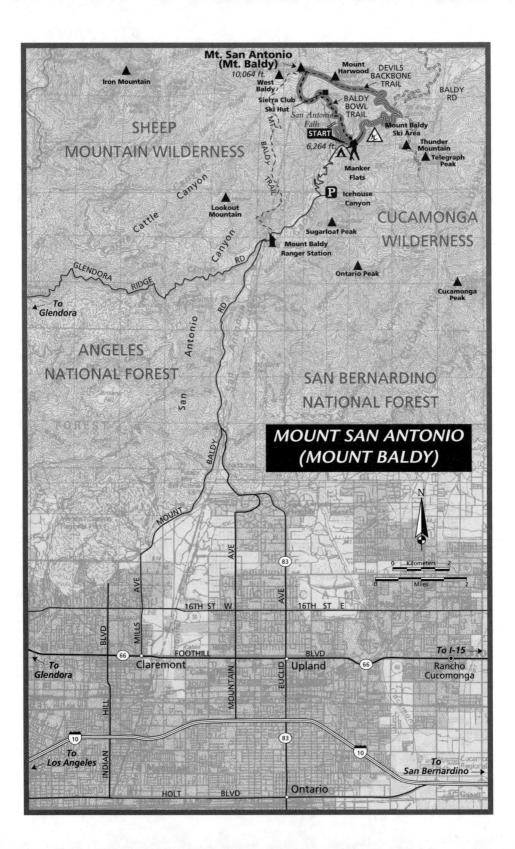

Devils Backbone, Mount San Antonio

Maps: USGS Mount San Antonio; DeLorme *Southern California Atlas and Gazetteer*, page 94; Tom Harrison, Angeles High Country.

Latitude: 34°17'20"N

Longitude: 117°38'45"W

Permits: None needed; day use only. In addition, a pass (Adventure Pass) is necessary for parking (available at state and federal ranger stations).

Trailhead: From Interstate 10 in Claremont, exit on Mountain Avenue and drive north, following the sign to the avenue's junction with Mount Baldy Road. Follow Mount Baldy Road 11 miles to Manker Campground. The trailhead is 0.3 mile up the road from the campground, on the left.

Mount San Antonio, or Mount Baldy as it is often called, is a refreshing oasis in the midst of the Los Angeles urban sprawl. The route described is a loop, chosen for its variety of terrain and eclectic biotic zones. This route combines the Baldy Bowl Trail (also known as the Ski Hut Trail) for the ascent, with the Devils Backbone Trail and Manker Canyon Fire Trail for the descent.

From the trailhead, hike up a fire road toward San Antonio Falls, which come into view after about half a mile (a short side trail leads to the base of the falls). Back on the fire road, the pavement ends shortly after the falls. A little farther, the trail toward the summit leaves the fire road. Keep a sharp watch to the left, as this much smaller trail, the Baldy Bowl Trail, is easy to miss. From the road the trail is very steep. Fortunately, fir trees and Jeffrey pines provide some shade.

About 2.5 miles from the trailhead, you'll reach a Sierra Club hut. Past the hut, the trail crosses a creek, then becomes less distinct as it goes through a boulder field before switchbacking up a wooded section on the other side. A ridge at the top of the switchbacks marks the transition from trees to manzanita.

Various trails, some marked with cairns, lead up through this next section. A little less than a mile farther, they converge on a gravelly slope leading to the summit plateau. From the summit you can see greater Los Angeles, the San Bernardino and San Gabriel Mountains, the Mojave Desert and, on a very clear day, Catalina Island.

To continue the loop hike, descend to the east down the rocky Devils Backbone Trail through limber pines to a saddle. Below, the sharp ridgeline known as the Devils Backbone connects Mount Baldy with Mount Harwood. South (right) is San Antonio Canyon and to the north is the Lytle Creek drainage.

After Devils Backbone, follow a road that is used seasonally by the Mount Baldy Ski Area. Occasional incense cedars shade the 1.3-mile stroll down to Baldy Notch. At the bottom of this ski run you arrive at a chairlift (which continues operation on weekends throughout the summer).

The Manker Canyon Fire Trail leads down from here. Tree-shaded but steep, this hike descends for 3 miles to the ski area parking lot. From there it is a walk of less than half a mile down the main road and back to the trailhead.

66. SAN JACINTO PEAK

Highlights: Clean, white granite boulders, rock climbing, fabulous views. And the largest pine cones you'll probably ever see.
Distance: 11 miles round trip (all trail).
Difficulty: Class 2; strenuous.
Trailhead Elevation: 6,560 feet
Summit Elevation: 10,804 feet
Elevation Gain: 4,244 feet
Best Months: May through October.
Maps: USGS San Jacinto Peak; DeLorme *Southern California Atlas and Gazetteer*, page 106.
Latitude: 33°48'52"N
Longitude: 116°40'42"W
Permits: California wilderness permit is needed for all hiking (available at the Idyllwild ranger station). In addition, a pass (Adventure Pass) is necessary for parking (available at state and federal ranger stations).
Trailhead: Marion Mountain Campground. From Idyllwild, take Route 243 north for 2 miles to the Alandale ranger station. Turn east at Stone Creek Campground and drive 3 miles to Marion Mountain Campground. The trailhead, signed for Marion Mountain, is at a small pullout on the right, near an old concrete water-containment structure.

John Muir called the view from the summit of San Jacinto Peak "one of the most sublime spectacles to be found on earth." It's true. You'll be seeing vistas all the

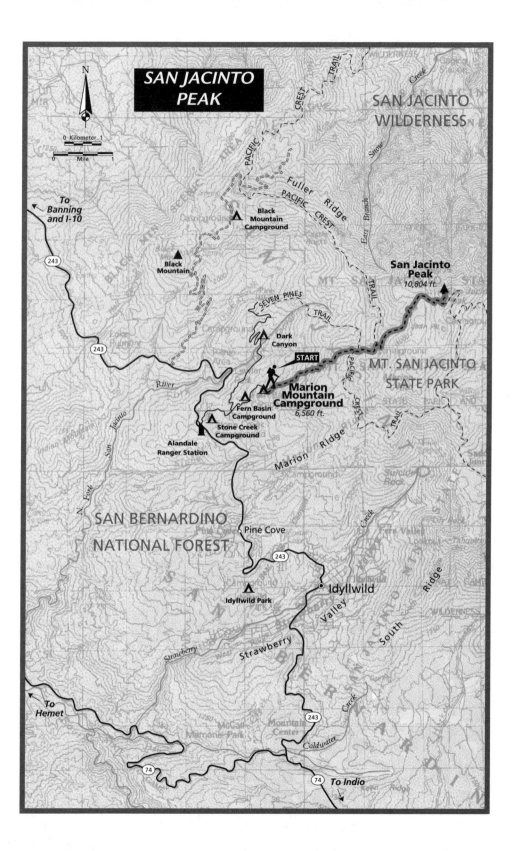

SAN JACINTO
PEAK

N

0 Kilometer 1

0   Mile   1

SAN JACINTO
WILDERNESS

To
Banning
and I-10

243

Fuller Ridge

PACIFIC CREST

East Branch

Snow Creek

Creek

Black
Mountain
Campground

Black
Mountain

San Jacinto
Peak
10,804 ft.

243

SEVEN PINES
TRAIL

Dark
Canyon

START

Marion
Mountain
Campground
6,560 ft.

PACIFIC CREST TRAIL

MT. SAN JACINTO
STATE PARK

River

Fern Basin
Campground

Stone Creek
Campground

Alandale
Ranger Station

San Jacinto

N. Fork

Marion Ridge

Pine Cove

SAN BERNARDINO
NATIONAL FOREST

243

Idyllwild

Valley

South Ridge

Idyllwild Park

To
Hemet

Strawberry

Strawberry

Creek

Coldwater

243

McCall
Memorial Park

Mountain
Center

74

74

To Indio

way from Nevada to the Pacific Ocean, from Mexico to the Sierra. This is a long day hike, or an overnighter with a stay at Round Valley Camp.

From the trailhead, climb a steep, heavily wooded hillside to a junction with the Pacific Crest Trail, 2 miles into the hike. Leaving the Crest Trail behind, stay on the ascent trail for another mile, to its junction with the Deer Springs Trail. (Before this junction, be sure to bear right at an earlier junction with the Seven Pines Trail.)

Follow the Deer Springs Trail north, through deep woods, switchbacks, and creek crossings. Stay on the Deer Springs Trail (bear right) at its junction with the Fuller Ridge Trail. From here, wide switchbacks through wooded boulder fields take you past Little Round Valley Camp to the junction with the San Jacinto Peak Trail. From here it's a quarter-mile to the top. Climb past a stone building to the rocky summit.

If you're a climber, don't forget your shoes. The entire summit area is a bouldering mecca regularly visited by climbers escaping the desert heat.

67. SAN GORGONIO MOUNTAIN

Highlights: Views from the desert to the Pacific.
Distance: 14 miles round trip (all trail).
Difficulty: Class 1; strenuous.
Trailhead Elevation: 6,199 feet
Summit Elevation: 11,149 feet
Elevation Gain: 4,950 feet
Best Months: May through October.
Maps: USGS San Gorgonio Mountain; DeLorme *Southern California Atlas and Gazetteer*, page 96.
Latitude: 34°06'02"N
Longitude: 116°49'40"W
Permits: Wilderness permit is needed for all hiking (available at Mill Creek Ranger Station, on Highway 38 just east of the town of Mentone). In addition, a pass (Adventure Pass) is necessary for parking (available at state and federal ranger stations).
Trailhead: Vivian Creek Trailhead. From Interstate 10, exit in Redlands and follow Highway 38 east. At about 7 miles is the Mill Creek Ranger Station, just past Mentone. Seven miles farther is the junction with Forest Home Road; continue straight on Valley of the Falls Drive for 4.5 miles to the trailhead at the end of the road.

San Gorgonio Mountain makes for a long day; start early or plan to camp along the way. Though the trailhead is obvious, the trail itself is indistinct for the first three-quarters of a mile, due to use trails and summer cabins.

You're on the right path when you cross the rocky Mill Creek wash and ascend an abrupt, steep trail on the other side, the north side. After a short distance, Vivian Creek Trail Camp is reached. The trail then follows Vivian Creek, wandering under Jeffrey pines and incense cedars.

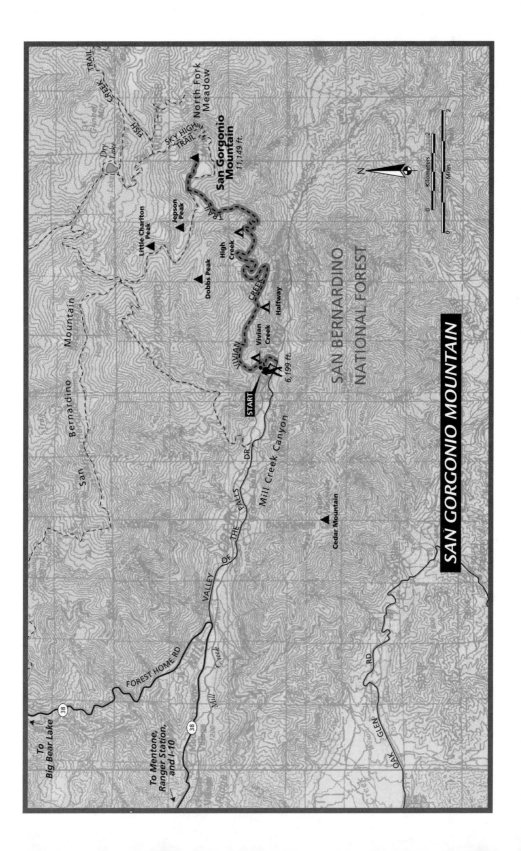

SAN GORGONIO MOUNTAIN

A few miles farther, a sign marked "Halfway" announces Halfway Camp. The camp is halfway between Vivian Creek Trail Camp and High Creek Camp. To the chagrin of tired hikers, it is not quite halfway to the summit.

After High Creek Camp the forest opens up. Two miles farther is the junction with Sky High Trail, at 11,200 feet. From here you can see Mount San Jacinto. The summit of San Gorgonio is a little less than a mile farther. Dirt trail gives way to the summit rocks.

68. CLARK MOUNTAIN

Highlights: A desert peak easily accessible from Highway 15. This is a mountain that you can bag on the otherwise monotonous drive from Los Angeles to Las Vegas. Clark Mountain is the high point of Mojave National Preserve.

Distance: 2.5 miles round trip (half on trail, half off trail).

Difficulty: Class 3; easy.

Trailhead Elevation: 6,000 feet

Summit Elevation: 7,929 feet

Elevation Gain: 1,929 feet

Best Months: October through May.

Maps: Clark Mountain; DeLorme *Southern California Atlas and Gazetteer*, page 57.

Latitude: 35°31'31"N

Longitude: 115°35'18"W

Permits: None needed. However, a pass (Adventure Pass) is necessary for parking (available at state and federal ranger stations).

Trailhead: Take the Mountain Pass exit off Interstate 15, about 16 miles west of the Nevada border. From here drive north several hundred yards, turn left, and drive about a mile, past the Caltrans compound, and then another half-mile to a junction. At the junction, turn right and drive a half-mile, turn left, and follow a power-line road for 1.8 miles. Two lefts lead to switchbacks up a canyon, and the road ends at a picnic area 4 miles from the highway. A high-clearance vehicle is recommended.

Clark Mountain is a refreshing climb out of the desert. From the picnic area at the trailhead, climb to a saddle, bypassing a dry waterfall. Follow a dry creek bed, first down and then up, toward the prominent limestone cliff. Follow the weakness in the cliff to the ridge, requiring Class 3 climbing. From the top of the cliff, follow a use trail left to the summit.

Clark Mountain is becoming an increasingly popular destination for rock climbers from Las Vegas and Southern California.

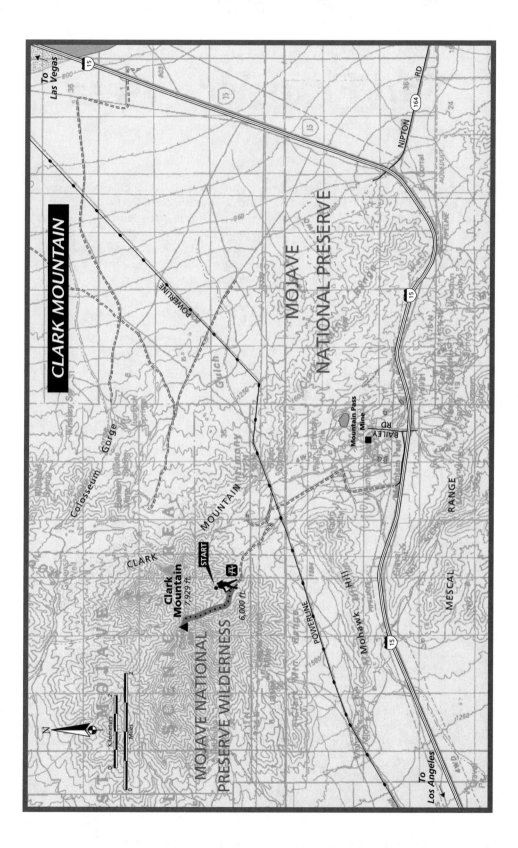

CLARK MOUNTAIN

N

Kilometers
Miles

To
Las Vegas

To
Las Vegas

To
Los Angeles

MOJAVE NATIONAL
PRESERVE WILDERNESS

MOJAVE NATIONAL PRESERVE

Colosseum
Gorge

POWERLINE

CLARK

MOUNTAIN

Clark
Mountain
7,929 ft.

START

6,000 ft.

POWERLINE

Mohawk Hill

MESCAL
RANGE

Mountain Pass
Mine

BAILEY RD

BAILEY RD

NIPTON RD

San Francisco Area

The San Francisco Bay Area is a large metropolitan area that includes a good deal of open space. Mount Tamalpais and Muir Woods in Marin County, just north of San Francisco, provide hiking opportunities. But it is the East Bay, with the rambling Contra Costa hills and trail system, that offers the most hiking—and the only true mountain in the area. With more than 3,000 feet of vertical relief, Mount Diablo can be seen for 50 or more miles in all directions. It is a big peak, relative to its surroundings, and dominates the scene.

69. MOUNT DIABLO

Highlights: A high point in the low-lying San Francisco Bay Area, with views of the bay, Mount Tamalpais and, on a clear day, Mount Lassen and the Sierra Nevada.
Distance: 2.6-mile loop (all trail).
Difficulty: Class 1; easy.
Trailhead Elevation: 3,069 feet
Summit Elevation: 3,849 feet
Elevation Gain: 780 feet
Best Months: Accessible year-round, but midsummer can be hot.
Maps: USGS Clayton; DeLorme *Northern California Atlas and Gazetteer*, page 105.
Latitude: 37°52'54"N
Longitude: 121°54'46"W
Permits: None needed; day use only; park entrance fee is charged.
Trailhead: Laurel Nook Group Picnic Area in Juniper Campground. From I-680 in Walnut Creek, take the Ygnacio Valley Road exit and drive east on this road for 2.6 miles to Walnut Avenue, and turn right. Take Walnut for 1.5 miles to Oak Grove Road and turn right, then take an immediate left onto North Gate Road. Follow this increasingly steep and windy road for 10.5 miles to the Juniper Campground; the Laurel Nook Picnic Area is on a bend of the outer loop.

Views from Mount Diablo are widespread, from the Farallon Islands west of San Francisco to the Sierra and north to Mount Lassen. Start on the dirt trail at Laurel Nook Group Picnic Area. This graded trail was built by the Youth Conservation Corps in 1977. Hike first in the open, then under a canopy of laurels and oaks.

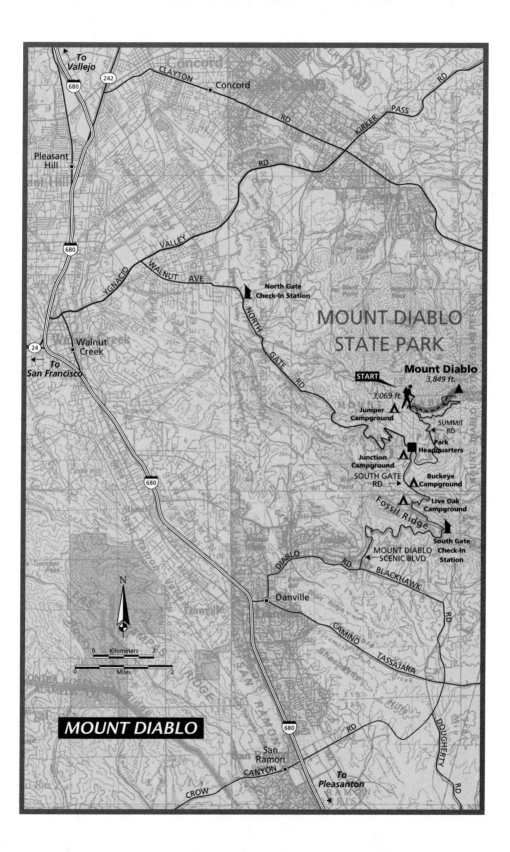

Switchbacks wind up to Moses Rock Ridge. Head right, through heavy brush and past rocky outcrops. Soon the trail crosses the summit road and enters the parking lot; follow uphill to the visitor center. Climb the outside stairs to the very summit, with its shaded pavilion, and look at the 360-degree panorama of ocean foothills and mountains.

Peaks at a Glance

		Summit Elevation (High Pt.)	Elevation Gain	Round-Trip Mileage	Class	Difficulty
NORTHERN CALIFORNIA						
1.	Mount Shasta	14,162	7,362	14	3	strenuous
2.	Castle Dome	4,700	1,950	6	3	moderate
3.	Mount Lassen	10,457	2,004	5	2	moderate
4.	Eureka Peak	7,497	1,997	6.6	2	moderate
5.	Sierra Buttes	8,591	1,579	5.2	2	easy/moderate
LAKE TAHOE AREA						
6.	Castle Peak	9,103	1,303	5.4	2	easy/moderate
7.	PCT Traverse	8,949	- - -	15.2*	2	strenuous
8.	Mount Tallac	9,740	3,340	10	2	strenuous
9.	Mount Rose	10,776	1,976	12	2	strenuous
10.	Freel Peak	10,881	2,461	8	2	moderate/strenuous
11.	Jobs Peak	10,673	2,253	12	2	strenuous
12.	Jobs Sister	10,823	2,403	10	2	strenuous
	Linkup: Freel/Jobs Peak/ Jobs Sister	10,823	- - -	13	2	strenuous
YOSEMITE NATIONAL PARK						
13.	Matterhorn Peak	12,279	5,187	8	2	moderate/strenuous
14.	Mount Conness	12,590	2,590	10.4	3	strenuous
15.	Mount Dana	13,057	3,067	5.8	2	moderate
16.	Amelia Earhart Peak	11,974	3,224	14	2	moderate
17.	Mount Lyell	13,114	4,364	23	3	very strenuous
18.	Mount Maclure	11,974	3,224	25	3	strenuous
	Linkup: Lyell/Maclure	13,114	- - -	- - -	3	very strenuous
19.	Cathedral Peak	10,911	2,211	6	4	moderate
20.	Clouds Rest					
	from Tuolumne Meadows	9,926	1,226	24*	2+	strenuous
	from Tenaya Lake	9,926	1,774	15*	2+	strenuous
	from Tenaya Lake	9,926	1,774	11†	2+	moderate
	from Yosemite Valley	9,926	6,026	20†	2+	strenuous
21.	Half Dome	8,836	4,936	16	3	moderate
HIGH SIERRA						
22.	Mammoth Mountain	11,053	2,053	8	2	easy
23.	Mount Ritter	13,157	4,757	9	3	strenuous
24.	Banner Peak	12,945	4,545	9	3	strenuous
	Linkup: Ritter/Banner	13,157	- - -	- - -	3	strenuous
25.	Mount Morrison	12,268	4,647	8	3	moderate
26.	Mount Starr	12,835	3,140	4.4	2	moderate
27.	Mount Morgan	13,748	4,053	9.6	3	moderate
28.	Mount Mills	13,468	3,773	8.2	3	moderate/strenuous
29.	Mount Abbot	13,704	4,009	8.4	3	strenuous
30.	Mount Dade	13,600	3,905	8.8	2-3	strenuous
31.	Mount Tom	13,652	5,652	14	2	strenuous
32.	Basin Mountain	13,240	5,240	13.5	2	moderate
33.	Mount Emerson	13,204	3,804	13	3	strenuous

34.	Mount Lamarck	13,417	4,017	12	2	moderate
35.	Mount Darwin	13,831	4,703	20	3	strenuous
36.	Hurd Peak	12,237	2,469	7	3	moderate
37.	Mount Gayley	13,510	5,510	15	3	strenuous
38.	Split Mountain	14,058	7,658	18	3	strenuous
39.	Mount Prater	13,329	6,929	14	3	strenuous
	Linkup: Split Mountain/Prater	14,058	- - -	16	3	strenuous
40.	Birch Mountain	13,665	7,265	13	2	strenuous
41.	Mount Tinemaha	12,561	6,161	5	2	moderate

MOUNT WHITNEY AREA

42.	Kearsarge Peak	12,598	3,398	4	2	easy/moderate
43.	Mount Williamson	14,375	8,775	30	3	very strenuous
44.	Mount Tyndall	14,018	8,418	30	2	strenuous
	Linkup: Williamson/Tyndall	14,375	- - -	- - -	3	very strenuous
45.	Mount Whitney					
	Main Whitney Trail	14,494	6,094	21	1	strenuous
	Mountaineer's Route	14,494	6,094	15	3	strenuous
46.	Mount Muir	14,015	5,615	17	3	strenuous
	Linkup: Whitney/Muir	14,494	- - -	22	3	strenuous
47.	Mount Russell	14,086	5,686	12	3	strenuous
48.	Lone Pine Peak	12,944	4,544	11	2	moderate/strenuous
49.	Mount LeConte	13,960	5,560	10	3	moderate
50.	Mount Mallory	13,850	5,450	9	2	moderate
51.	Mount Irvine	13,770	5,370	9	2	moderate
	Linkup: LeConte/Mallory/Irvine	13,960	- - -	13	3	very strenuous
52.	Mount Langley	14,042	3,642	21	2	moderate
53.	Cirque Peak	12,990	2,590	16	2	moderate
	Linkup: Langley/Cirque	14,042	- - -	27	2	strenuous
54.	Olancha Peak	12,124	6,324	13	3	strenuous

WEST OF THE SIERRA CREST

55.	Fresno Dome	7,540	540	1.6	1	easy
56.	Sawtooth Peak	12,343	4,543	12	2	moderate/strenuous
57.	Needham Mountain	12,467	4,667	13	2	moderate/strenuous
	Linkup: Sawtooth/ Needham	12,467	4,667	13	2	moderate/strenuous
58.	Mineral Peak	11,615	3,815	12	2	moderate/strenuous

WHITE MOUNTAINS AND DEATH VALLEY

59.	White Mountain Peak	12,246	2,246	14	2	moderate
60.	Waucoba Mountain	11,123	3,123	6	2	moderate
61.	Squaw Peak	10,358	2,358	4	2	moderate
	Linkup: Waucoba/Squaw	11,123	- - -	9††	2	moderate
62.	Wildrose Peak	9,064	2,164	8.4	2	moderate
63.	Telescope Peak	11,049	2,929	14	2	moderate/strenuous

SOUTHERN CALIFORNIA

64.	Mount Baden-Powell	9,399	2,843	8	2	easy
65.	Mount San Antonio	10,064	3,800	11††	2	strenuous
66.	San Jacinto Peak	10,804	4,244	11	2	strenuous
67.	San Gorgonio Mountain	11,149	4,950	14	1	strenuous
68.	Clark Mountain	7,929	1,929	2.5	3	easy

SAN FRANCISCO AREA

69.	Mount Diablo	3,849	780	2.6††	1	easy

* one-way, † round-trip, †† loop